Conten

Building
A
Eucharistic Community

A Handbook for Liturgical Catechesis

Mary J. McDonald

Resource Publications, Inc.
San Jose, California

Reprint Department
Resource Publications, Inc.
160 E. Virginia Street #290
San Jose, CA 95112-5876
(408) 286-8505 (voice)
(408) 287-8748 (fax)

Library of Congress Cataloging-in-Publication Data
McDonald, Mary J., 1930–
Building a Eucharistic community : a handbook for liturgical
catechesis / Mary J. McDonald.
   p.   cm.
Includes bibliographical references.
ISBN 0–89390–533–X (pbk.)
   1. Catechetics—Catholic Church. 2. Catholic Church—Liturgy.
I. Title.
BX1968 .M395 2001
268.82—dc21

                                                              2001019613

Printed in the United States of America.
01 02 03 04 05 | 5 4 3 2 1

Editorial director: Nick Wagner
Production: Romina Saha
Copyeditor: Leah Faltus
Cover design: Mike Sagara, Nelson Estarija
Cover photograph: Skjold Photographs

Introduction

Catholics through the ages have recognized the centrality of the eucharistic liturgy, the Mass, to a life of faith. In our own time, the Second Vatican Council, in its *Constitution on the Sacred Liturgy*, declared the liturgy to be "the summit toward which the activity of the Church is directed" and the "fount from which all [her] power flows" (10). The document insisted that the assembly's full participation in the liturgical celebration must be the primary purpose of the liturgy's restoration. The Council's choice of the word "restoration" underlines the fact that in earlier centuries the assembly's involvement was not in question.

The Eucharist, then, should be at the very heart of the life of the Christian community. This does not mean only that the whole parish will gather at the Sunday celebration. Rather, it suggests that "eucharistic living" will be the norm every day of the week. Bringing with them all that they are and offering themselves to the Father in union with the sacrifice of Christ, the community enters deeply into the paschal mystery, collectively and individually. Strengthened at the Lord's table, they are sent forth again to minister, to continue Christ's work and be Eucharist to others. This cycle is repeated again and again.

Liturgical catechesis is not, as might be assumed, catechesis *about* the eucharistic celebration, though this will be a small part of it. Instead, it is a process that is centered on the liturgy and grows out of the Sunday celebration itself, at the same time fostering more active participation. It becomes the way people of all ages are formed in faith. Perhaps this statement may sound a little vague. "What about curriculum," the reader may be thinking. "What about systematic doctrinal instruction? What age groups are targeted?" Some may even wonder, "Is this another newfangled idea that will erode the base of Catholic belief?"

It is my hope that these questions are satisfactorily answered, along with others, in the course of the book. To address them very briefly here:

- There is no curriculum in the accepted sense of the word, but the structure of the catechetical process is based on the seasons of the liturgical year.
- The learning of doctrine flows very naturally from the themes of the weekly Scripture readings.
- There are no age requirements; the church's catechetical documents of recent years unanimously affirm that catechesis should be lifelong and directed toward the ongoing conversion of every member of the Body of Christ. Therefore, it is a process of formation rather than a program of instruction.

The aim of liturgical catechesis is not only to turn out children, teens, or adults who are religiously literate; it is to form them into disciples of Jesus Christ, who live the values of the Gospel and work to build up the kingdom of God. Far from eroding belief, it builds up faith in heart and soul as well as head. This type of holistic formation conforms very closely to the catechumenal model of catechesis prescribed for the whole church by the recently issued *General Directory for Catechesis*. But it is not new. In fact, it is a restoration of the catechetical model that was the norm in the early centuries of Christianity.

The venerable Latin axiom *lex orandi, lex credendi* (which may be translated "the way we pray is the way we believe") attests to the fact that catechesis has been traditionally recognized as an important element of the liturgy. In 1963, Vatican II affirmed this understanding: "Although the liturgy is above all things the worship of the divine majesty, it likewise contains rich instruction for the faithful" (CSL 33). The following year, what was then the Sacred Congregation of Rites issued an *Instruction on the Proper Implementation of the Constitution on the Sacred Liturgy*, which states that the *Constitution*'s aim was "to foster the formation of the faithful and that pastoral activity of which the liturgy is the summit and source" (5).

Those called to the catechetical ministry desire to provide the type of Christian formation that will best help those they catechize to grow in faith and holiness. Unfortunately, in the years since Vatican II, there has been much disagreement in the catechetical community about the best ways in which this formation can be achieved. The *General Directory for Catechesis* deplores the fact that sometimes "tendentious positions have been adopted and set in opposition to the interpretation and application of the renewal sought by the Church"; as a result we have witnessed "divisions which damage that witness of communion indispensable to evangelization" (28).

It is to be hoped that the promulgation of the *General Directory for Catechesis* will begin a process of healing and reconciliation, so the church may have a more unified approach to catechesis. I hope that this handbook may, in a small way, contribute to such resolution of differences. This book is the fruit of many years of association with catechesis at many levels, during which I have been privileged to work as both a catechist and a leader in the catechetical ministry.

The handbook is intended to offer encouragement and guidance in the formation of a eucharistic community through a holistic approach to catechesis. It briefly highlights some elements of the *Constitution on the Sacred Liturgy*, and it offers a short overview of catechesis in the church through the centuries. We travel with a catechumen through the process of Christian initiation, the process that is to be the paradigm for all catechesis, and visit a lectionary-based catechetical session for children. In other chapters, I discuss the stages of faith formation and the importance of symbolic ritual both in worship and in deepening faith. Suggestions are also offered for incorporating many types of prayer experiences into the catechetical process. An outline of the factors involved in the formation of liturgical catechists draws heavily on the section of the *General Directory for Catechesis* that is devoted to this important topic. The final chapter gives a thumbnail sketch of a parish community centered on the Eucharist. It also outlines some strategies that may be helpful in building up and nurturing such a community.

Acknowledgments

My very grateful thanks go to many people who have contributed in some way to the writing of this book. I am particularly indebted to Sister Alice Mary Buckley, CCVI, EdD; Barbara Fleischer, PhD; Father Patrick J. Madden, PhD; and Father Thomas Ranzino, all of whom read the manuscript and contributed many helpful insights and suggestions. Special thanks go also to my editor, Nick Wagner, for his ongoing help and his patience, and to Sister Mary Ellen Theriot, SSND, Director of Religious Education for the Diocese of Alexandria, for her generous sharing of ideas and resources. Lastly, I would like to thank my family, whose love and encouragement have supported me, not just in the writing of this book but throughout my years of ministry.

Finally, grateful acknowledgment is extended to the copyright holders who granted permission to reprint the following material:

Excerpts from *Vatican Council II, Volume 1, Revised Edition: The Conciliar & Post Conciliar Documents* edited by Austin Flannery, O.P. copyright ©1998, Costello Publishing Company, Inc., Northport, NY are used by permission of the publisher, all rights reserved. No part of these excerpts may be reproduced, stored in a retrieval system, or transmitted in any form or by any means—electronic, mechanical, photo-copying, recording or otherwise, without express permission of Costello Publishing Company.

Scripture excerpts in this work are taken from the *New American Bible with Revised New Testament and Revised Psalms* © 1991, 1986, 1970 Confraternity of Christian Doctrine, Washington, D.C. Used with permission. All rights reserved. No part of the *New American Bible* may be reproduced in any form without permission in writing from the copyright owner.

1. The Liturgy

Discussion Questions

For Catechists

- What has been your recent experience of catechesis in your parish? Is it oriented toward encouraging more understanding of, and participation in the liturgy?

For Liturgists

- In what ways—through music, art, environment and ritual—could you foster the understanding that eucharistic celebrations are to continue outside the church building in works of service?

If someone were to ask a randomly picked group of Catholics how often each of them celebrates Sunday Mass, the answers might well vary all the way from "every week" to "sometimes" or "rarely." Yet all of them would consider themselves members of the church.

Readers of this book will probably agree with this assessment. Most of us have encountered teenagers who are vocal about their perception of Sunday Mass—"b-o-r-r-ring"—and younger children who seek for ways to avoid attending their parish liturgy. Their parents often are not present, or, if they are, yawn their way through their weekly obligation. They consult their watches at frequent intervals, seeming to believe that mere physical presence at the Sunday celebration is enough to fulfill this rather tedious duty.

In the days before the Second Vatican Council, by contrast, Catholic churches were packed at every Mass. However, although many people attended without fail because of a deep devotion to the Mass, research and personal conversations suggest that a considerable number were present for other reasons. Some were cultural: If you were Polish or Italian or Irish, you went to Mass on Sundays; it was a given. Other reasons had to do with the punishment (hell) for unrepented mortal sin. For still other people, churchgoing had become a long-established habit. Clearly, for countless numbers of Catholics, then as now, the liturgy had no profound meaning. In no way was it, or is it now, at the center of a Catholic's life, in some cases not even at the periphery. So the problem is not a new one.

Liturgical Renewal and Reform

Recognizing that action to renew the liturgy was necessary, the Second Vatican Council, in its first document, the *Constitution on the Sacred Liturgy*, mandated wide ranging changes in the manner in which the Mass was celebrated, based on the historical research and theological insights of the past fifty years. Some understanding of the problems facing the Council may be gained from the opening pages of the document. "Something more is required than the ... laws governing valid and lawful celebration"; pastors must "ensure that the faithful take part fully aware of what they are doing" (11); full participation "is the aim to be considered before all else" (14). "Thus to achieve the reform, progress, and adaptation of the liturgy, it is essential to promote that warm and living love for Scripture" (24). It is reasonable to suppose that all these elements of the liturgy—punctilious concern for details of the rubrics rather than for the spirit of the liturgy; lack of understanding of the liturgy and of full participation; lack of familiarity with and love for the Scriptures—were seen by the Council fathers as basic problems needing to be addressed.

Though the movement for liturgical renewal was gathering momentum long before the bishops of the world ever assembled in Rome in 1963, the scope and content of the changes in liturgical celebration that the Council mandated came upon the church suddenly, or so it seemed. They caught many of us unprepared. The liturgical reform was a "catechetical moment."

It was an opportunity to begin anew, so that everyone would gradually come to understand the true meaning of the eucharistic liturgy and to enter deeply into the mysteries. But the moment was lost. Pastors attempted to explain the details of the liturgical reforms. We learned the acclamations in which we were to join, the newly named parts of the Mass, and the practices that had been introduced—the offering of the sign of peace, the new way to receive the Eucharist; when to stand, sit, and kneel. The majority of Catholics seem to have adapted to these external modifications without understanding why they had been introduced, or interiorizing the deep inner meaning they signified. On the contrary, in rather sheep-like fashion, many obediently followed the new set of instructions without asking questions.

I remember an elderly man from my parish who attended a diocesan-sponsored course on the liturgy in the early 1980s (already fifteen years after the Council closed). The instructor suggested that the *Constitution on the Sacred Liturgy* based its directives on a renewed theology of Eucharist, recovering some aspects that had been lost over the centuries.

"Oh, I don't agree with that at all," the man said, quite indignantly. "I think everything is just the same except that the altar is turned around and we can understand the prayers now that they're in English." He was typical of countless Catholics of that time, and even of many today. Change is often very difficult, especially when it involves deeply cherished beliefs and practices. Failure, or inability, to change often hardens into non-involvement and isolation.

Understanding the Liturgy

In the past several years, a number of U.S. bishops have written pastoral letters aimed at explaining the theology and spirituality of the Eucharist more fully. They have been concerned that the celebration of parish liturgies often lacks the spirit and power that comes from understanding and full participation. So far, the vision and bright promise of the *Constitution on the Sacred Liturgy* has not come to full fruition. We have not yet plumbed the riches of the liturgical renewal, and, with notable exceptions, the vibrant, faith-filled liturgies envisaged by the Council fathers are still the stuff of dreams.

With hindsight, many of us who experienced the first days of the reformed liturgy recognize that the catechesis we received should have been more detailed and prolonged. But, like the pastors themselves, the catechetical community was busy with implementing the new approaches implied in the vast scope of the Council documents and later spelled out more explicitly in a number of church documents. However that may be, it is obvious that the present situation presents a major challenge to all those involved in the ministry of catechesis. But it is not too late.

The *Constitution on the Sacred Liturgy* declared unequivocally that, "The liturgy is the summit toward which the activity of the Church is directed; ... it is the fount from which all [her] power flows" (10). Given this understanding, it is not surprising that the Council fathers mandated changes designed to facilitate "that full, conscious and active participation in liturgical celebrations called for by the very nature of the liturgy" and to which the Christian people have a "right and duty by reason of their baptism." The liturgy is "the primary and indispensable source from which the faithful are to derive the true Christian spirit" (14).

Clearly, then, the liturgy must be at the very heart of our life of faith. All of us in the Catholic community are both entitled and obligated to participate in it to the full, and to take whatever means are needed to understand it as completely as we are able. It is only if we do these things that we will be filled with the "true Christian spirit" that will enable us to go forth in mission—to live the paschal mystery of Christ's death and resurrection in daily life. If we choose to put our all into the celebration, we will encounter the risen Lord and will be transformed. But if we choose to participate only superficially and marginally, we will be effectively blocking the action of the Holy Spirit. In so doing, we will fail in our obligation both to God and to the worshiping community.

The word *liturgy* means "the prescribed rites used for public worship." In the Catholic and Orthodox traditions, it usually refers to the Mass, though it can also be used to describe any sacramental rituals. The word is derived from the Greek *leitourgia*, which may be translated as "the work of the people." The liturgy, then, is never something the priest does while we respond from time to time with a set formula such as, "And also with you," "Praise to you, Lord Jesus Christ," or "Amen." It is always something that presider and assembly do together, the public action of the whole worshiping community. Additionally, the liturgy is not a series of prayers interspersed by other activities, such as singing, listening to the scripture readings, or saying the Creed. The whole liturgical celebration is one continuous prayer.

It is of the utmost importance to realize that, at each liturgy, Christ is present in the gathered community, in the ministers, and in the Scriptures, as well as in the eucharistic species. In the Liturgy of the Word, Christ himself speaks to us, through the biblical readings and in the homily. The introduction to the new lectionary, issued in 1999, reminds us that "the divine word read and proclaimed by the Church in the Liturgy has as its one purpose the sacrifice of the New Covenant and the banquet of grace, that is, the Eucharist. The celebration of Mass, in which the word is heard and the Eucharist is offered and received, forms but one single act of divine worship" (10).

In the Liturgy of the Eucharist, the paschal mystery of Jesus' death and resurrection, through which God's final purpose for humanity was fulfilled, is actually *made present* to us. This is not a re-enactment, but a re-presentation, in which we enter with the risen Christ into the mystery so that we can be changed into "other Christs," who carry on the work the Lord began during his earthly ministry.

I recently attended a talk on the Eucharist and was surprised to discover that a considerable number of attendees believed that Christ actually dies again at each individual Mass. The bishop who was making the presentation took time to explain that this was not so, quoting Paul's statement in the letter to the Romans: "We know that Christ, raised from the dead, dies no more; death no longer has power over him" (Rom 6:9).

Paragraph 1085 of the *Catechism of the Catholic Church* explains that in the paschal mystery "Christ ... participates in the divine eternity, and so transcends all times while being made present in them all." Though the crucifixion and resurrection were historical events, they "cannot remain only in the past, because by his death he destroyed death." So, as the *Catechism* beautifully summarizes, "the event of the Cross and Resurrection *abides* and draws everything toward life." In other words, on each occasion when we participate in the eucharistic celebration, we encounter the eternal, risen Christ, who is no longer subject to human limitations of time and space. He is truly present in that particular time and location, as is *the whole saving event by which he overcame sin and death.* Christ has passed through death into the eternal "now" of God.

In participating in the liturgy, then, we share a moment in which time is taken up into eternity. Our sharing in the communion rite is truly a foretaste of the "feast of the Lamb," of which Revelation speaks—the heavenly banquet in which we all hope to participate at the end of our earthly life. "In the earthly liturgy we take part in a foretaste of the heavenly liturgy celebrated in the holy city of Jerusalem toward which we journey as pilgrims, where Christ is sitting at the right hand of God" (CSL 8).

However, it is not just for our own sanctification that we are invited to the table of the Lord's Word and of his Body. Partaking of bread and wine is a sign of the unity of all the baptized and of the renewal of the New Covenant between God and God's holy people. We, on our part, fulfill that covenant by going forth from the celebration to minister to others, strengthened by our participation in the sacrificial meal.

To participate with this understanding is not only to know and appreciate what is going on in the liturgy but to become personally involved in the prayers of praise, thanksgiving, repentance and petition, moments of silence, and all the symbolic rituals and actions of the celebration. This is an involvement of the whole person: body, mind, heart and spirit. Anyone who does not go forth "to love and serve the Lord in one another" in imitation of the total self-giving of Jesus has not fully participated in the eucharistic mystery. Our call is to evangelize, to build up God's reign of peace and justice, and to extend God's love to all people. We are to be the presence of Christ in our locality. Unfortunately, there are many in our assemblies who appear to be unaware of these aspects of the liturgy.

Catechesis and Liturgy Today

Pastors (and, of course, catechists) are called upon "with zeal and patience" to "promote the liturgical instruction of the faithful and also their active participation ... both internally and externally." In doing this they will be "fulfilling one of their chief duties as faithful stewards of the mysteries of God" (CSL 19).

If God is at the center of our personal and communal universe; if, as the church teaches, the liturgy is "the source and summit of the Christian life" (*Dogmatic Constitution on the Church* 11), how can we *not* bring the whole liturgical experience to the very heart of all our catechetical efforts?

"But what more can we do?" the catechist or DRE may say. "We try to teach the children about the Mass. Their religion books have a unit or two on Mass and the sacraments each year, and references to the liturgy in other lessons. We try to make a connection with the Sunday liturgy by asking them what the Scripture readings were about, but either they don't remember or they didn't go that week."

Somehow it seems that despite our best efforts, people simply do not make the connection between what we try to teach and the liturgies they attend, whether it be under duress, on Sundays—or, indeed, in the daily lives they live for the rest of the week. The impact we make sometimes seems to be minimal in terms of forming a close relationship with Christ, which results in lived Christianity or discipleship. The *General Directory for Catechesis*, issued in Rome by the Congregation for the Clergy in 1997, complains: "Frequently ... the practice of catechetics testifies to a weak and fragmentary link with the liturgy." The *Directory* cites insufficient attention to symbolic ritual, "little or no connection with the liturgical year," and "the marginalization of liturgical celebrations" as contributing factors to the problem (30).

Enter liturgical catechesis!

Liturgical catechesis is not just another catechetical tool to be added on to your existing program for children, youth, and adults. Where would you find time for that? It is not a program of instruction *about* the liturgy. Rather it is a process, a way to approach all catechesis that is *grounded in and permeated by the liturgy* as the source and summit of Christian life. It is a different way of catechizing, a different model or paradigm, a process of formation in Christian living, rather than a curriculum-based program. Though the *content* of the faith is still learned, the *context* for that learning is the Christian community assembled for worship rather than the classroom.

"Catechesis is intrinsically bound to every liturgical and sacramental action," notes the *General Directory for Catechesis* (30, quoting *Catechesi Tradendae* 23). The *Constitution on the Sacred Liturgy* itself declares, "Although the liturgy is above all things the worship of the divine majesty, it likewise contains rich instruction for the faithful" (33). This instruction comes through the readings and prayers, actions and gestures, rites and symbols of the eucharistic celebration. It is not surprising, therefore, that a catechesis that is called "liturgical" uses the liturgy itself as its text, with particular emphasis on the lectionary, the liturgical book from which the Scripture is proclaimed. Of course, it also incorporates all the key elements of Catholic teaching as these are suggested by the Scripture readings throughout the year.

As will be obvious, liturgical catechesis is not confined to children and adolescents. Rather, in accordance with all the catechetical documents of recent years, it also recognizes the need for lifelong spiritual growth and faith development through various forms of adult catechesis. Ultimately it involves the whole parish, forming it gradually into a eucharistic community and impacting the whole dynamic of parish ministry.

14

Best of all, liturgical catechesis closely reflects the catechetical model prescribed by the *General Directory for Catechesis*.

Probably an embodiment of this model already exists in your parish in the form of the baptismal catechumenate, the *Rite of Christian Initiation of Adults* or RCIA. This is, of course, a form of liturgical catechesis! To the joy of some (particularly those who have worked as catechumenate team members) and the dismay of others, the *General Directory for Catechesis* insists that *the catechumenate should be the model for all catechesis*. However, it states, there is "a fundamental difference ... between the *pre-baptismal* and the *post-baptismal* catechesis" (90) used for those who have already been initiated into the church, rather than for those preparing for baptism. Therefore, the structure of the catechumenate should not be "slavishly" (91) followed in every detail. Nevertheless, it contains basic elements that need to be universally applied. The formation given to those being catechized in the catechumenate "should inspire the other forms of catechesis in both their objectives and in their dynamism" (GDC 59).

In order to understand the full implications of the prescriptions of the *General Directory*, it will be necessary to examine in some detail the structure and dynamic of the baptismal catechumenate. Before doing so, however, it may be helpful to take a very brief look at the history of catechesis during the past two millennia. The next chapter will attempt to do this.

Discussion Question

For Catechists and Liturgists

- How do you understand the statement of the Second Vatican Council that the liturgy is the "source and summit of the Christian life"? In what practical ways could liturgists and catechists cooperate to increase awareness of the centrality of the liturgy?

2. Catechesis: Past and Present

Discussion Questions

For Catechists

- How do your understand your role as a catechist? What do you think is the most important aspect of your ministry?
- In your personal faith journey, has it been instruction in formal doctrine, or your own life experience, that has been the most influential factor in forming a relationship with God?

For Liturgists

- How and in what ways does the liturgy catechize? What is the relationship between worship and formation?

In giving workshops to beginning catechists, I often ask them: "How do you understand your ministry? Why have you volunteered to be a catechist."

Several people usually respond, "To teach children their faith" or "To help them understand Catholic teaching" or even "To help them defend their faith," as if these statements encapsulated everything that catechesis is about. Eventually someone will answer, "To help them get to know Jesus and to have a relationship with Jesus."

In the days before the Second Vatican Council, any one of the first three would have been the obvious answer—so obvious, in fact, that no one would ever think of asking the question! Many of us who grew up before Vatican II remember the "catechism classes" of our youth, in which we were required to recite memorized definitions of the key elements of Catholic belief. This material may have been supplemented to some degree by religious sisters and brothers who introduced a spiritual dimension, and, on rare occasions, shared with us some of their own faith experience. Of course, in many cases, parents (who, after all, are recognized by the church as the "primary educators" of their children) may have provided opportunities for prayer at home; and youth movements in the '50s and '60s taught various forms of prayer to their members. But for very many Catholics, living a Christian life basically meant "hearing" Mass, receiving the appropriate sacraments, and keeping the Ten Commandments. Prayer, for the most part, was understood as the recitation of learned formulas.

Catechesis in the First Christian Centuries

Things were not always so. In the early centuries after Christ, when most people becoming Christian were adults or whole families, people were initiated through the catechumenate, a process of conversion and formation which could last up to three years. It was understood that the entire community was to model lived faith through their everyday lives, prayer, and participation in the eucharistic liturgy, since everyone was responsible for the formation of catechumens, as they were called.

During liturgical celebrations, the story of salvation history was recounted through the reading and explanation of the Scriptures. This element of the process was regarded as of prime importance. When the catechumens participated with the community in liturgical rites or celebrations and worked alongside them in various types of ministry, they learned, by a kind of osmosis, what it meant to be a Christian in that place and time, in those particular circumstances, all within the framework of the whole Catholic tradition.

It was only as Easter approached, with the celebration of the initiation sacraments—baptism, confirmation and Eucharist—that basic doctrinal instruction was included. These consisted of explanations of the Creed, the Our Father, and moral teachings (GDC 89). The great and glorious event of the resurrection was uppermost in everyone's mind, so that catechesis was imbued with the concept of baptism, of dying with Christ, and rising to new life. A period of post-baptismal catechesis deepened the understanding of this mystery.

But fewer and fewer adult conversions occurred as time passed. By the eighth century, Christendom embraced the whole western world, as it was then known, and for the vast majority of people, travel to other regions was virtually non-existent. So almost everyone was baptized as an infant, and the catechumenate was no longer needed. It was not restored until 1963.

Catechesis in Medieval Times

In the early Middle Ages, very few people outside the monasteries and the royal courts were able to read. They were taught the Creed and basic prayers, and most of them were catechized by listening to the Scriptures (and the homily when there was one). They also participated in the liturgy. In churches throughout Christendom, statues, frescoes, stained glass windows, and mosaics brought to life the oft-repeated stories about the life, death and resurrection of Jesus; of Mary and the apostles; of characters in the Hebrew Scriptures; and of favorite saints. Although this type of formation could not compare with the comprehensive process of the catechumenate, the *locus* of catechesis was still the liturgical celebration in the midst of the faith community.

Consequences of the Reformation

It was not until the sixteenth century, when Luther and the other reformers posed a serious challenge to Catholic doctrine, that the Council of Trent (1545–63) authorized the publication of what came to be known as the "Roman Catechism." From this compendium of church teaching, small question-and-answer catechisms, providing useful summaries of key doctrines, were produced. The idea for such booklets originally came from Luther himself, who, using the recently invented printing press, developed them as an effective way to promulgate his beliefs. As the Catholic Church followed suit, the teaching of basic concepts by means of short, standard formulas became the universally accepted means of "instruction in the faith" for generations of children, until the time of the Second Vatican Council (1962–65).

This question-and-answer method was introduced partly to remedy the inadequacies of previous centuries, when little systematized learning of doctrine took place. At the same time, it was considered necessary to equip Catholics with a rudimentary knowledge of church teaching, in order to respond intelligently, and with conviction, to the dissemination of Protestant doctrines.

An unfortunate result of the method chosen was that the connection between liturgy and catechesis was largely lost, and "information" now took precedence over "formation."

Between Trent and Vatican II

The Council of Trent launched the Counter-Reformation in response to a particular set of circumstances—the teaching and practices of the Protestant reformers. But in the four hundred years following that council, many forces of change were at work. Numerous wars, culminating in two world-wide conflicts; the rise and fall of empires; the revival of the ancient Greek concept of the republic; the rise of communism; the industrial revolution and the subsequent technological revolution—all these radically changed every aspect of human life in Europe, and, eventually, in most parts of the world. Meanwhile, the Enlightenment had introduced new systems of philosophical thought which rejected many of the time-honored concepts and assumptions upon which medieval thinking was based.

The First Vatican Council met from 1869–70 to address some of the problems arising from the changing face of society. But by mid-twentieth century, the church was making less and less impact upon the unchurched, and even many of the faithful had drifted away. Life seemed to have lost meaning for count-less millions. The change in cultural, social, and economic con-ditions continued to accelerate, and with the expansion of research and scholarship, a resulting explosion of knowledge was threatening to sweep away the last vestiges of the old order. The prescriptions of Trent, successful though they had origi-nally been, were not meeting contemporary needs. In 1962, Pope John XXIII, "the caretaker pope" as he was called, sum-moned the bishops of the world together in the Second Vatican Council.

Vatican II

The Council, which Pope John Paul II has called "a providen-tial event," produced an "enormously rich body of teaching," presented in "a striking new tone," amounting to "a proclama-tion of new times" (*On the Coming of the Third Millennium* 18, 20). From the reform of the liturgy and sacramental rites to the demands of Christian living; from the church's self-understand-ing to missionary activity and ecumenism; from a greatly increased emphasis on the importance of Scripture to the need for the laity to transform the society in which they live, the Council catapulted the Catholic Church into the contemporary scene. The *Pastoral Constitution on the Church in the Modern World* outlines many of the church's responses to the cultural, social, and economic conditions of 1965, most of which are still with us. Among the numerous evils cited were: lack of respect for human life and dignity; social injustice resulting in poverty, hunger and disease; the arms race, and the indiscriminate destruction of cities and their inhabitants in war; arbitrary imprisonment, even slavery, and many more. The laity, the *Con-stitution* declared, "are to animate the world with the spirit of Christianity" as witnesses to Christ at the heart of the human community (43). A new challenge faced the catechetical pro-cess.

Even before the Council began its work, catechists were real-izing that all was not well in the way Catholic children and young people were being educated and trained in the faith. By and large, adults were not being catechized at all, since they had already been taught the catechism as children. The Council documents with their mandates for reform, renewal, and revitalization made it even more imperative to address this whole problem in a radical way.

Post-Conciliar Documents

The *General Catechetical Directory* of 1971 pointed out the need for a renewal of catechesis: "The faith of many Christians is strained to a critical point .... Great numbers are drifting little by little into religious indifferentism, or are continuing in danger of keeping the faith without the dynamism that is necessary, a faith without effective influence on their actual lives" (6).

The Vatican II Decree on the Office of Bishops in the Church had already mandated "a directory for the catechetical instruction of the Christian people in which the fundamental principles of this instruction and its organization will be dealt with" (44). When the *General Catechetical Directory* was published, it emphasized the need to move in new directions with catechesis, using a different methodology and giving more emphasis to spirituality. It also stressed the importance of connecting people's "more significant experiences, both personal and social," to the teaching of the Gospel and illuminating them in the light of revelation. "Experience can also help make the Christian message more intelligible." This, of course, is consistent with the teaching of Christ himself, who "preached the kingdom of God by illustrating its nature with parables drawn from the experience of human life" (74).

When we hear the word "catechesis," we usually think of it in terms of the formation of children or of people who desire to enter the church. The *General Catechetical Directory*, however, viewed it from a different perspective: "Catechesis for adults, since it deals with persons who are capable of an adherence that is fully responsible, must be considered the chief form of catechesis. All other forms ... are in some way oriented to it" (20). In 1979, the Catechetical Directory for the United States,

Sharing the Light of Faith, was issued, developing the themes of the *General Directory* and applying them to the American experience.

In the meantime, Pope Paul VI had issued his landmark encyclical, *On Evangelization in the Modern World*. Building on the insights of the Vatican Council, which declared the community of the church to be the people of God, Paul gave a new understanding and impetus to ecumenism, and renewed the understanding that the spreading of the Gospel was the mission of every member of the church. The pope explained evangelization as "bringing the Good News into all the strata of humanity, and through its influence transforming humanity from within" (18). He declared: "[The church] exists to evangelize" (14).

When John Paul II succeeded to the papacy in 1978, one of his first acts was to promulgate an apostolic exhortation entitled *On Catechesis in our Time*. He developed the thought of his predecessor, situating catechesis firmly within the process of evangelization, which, he wrote, "is made up of elements, or ... moments" that are interdependent. "Catechesis is one of these moments" (18). Catechesis, the pope declared, must always be centered on Christ. Its "definitive aim"—that which actually defines its nature—"is to put people not only in touch but in communion, in intimacy, with Jesus Christ: only He can lead us to the love of the Father in the Spirit and make us share in the life of the Holy Trinity" (5).

This was a major innovation for those who still believed that "passing on the faith" meant primarily teaching a series of doctrinal statements. Some twenty years later, John Paul's vision does not seem to have been fully accepted or understood by catechists. I recall giving a talk to a group of volunteers in a small, rather conservative parish, trying to impress upon them what the Pope's statement might mean in concrete terms. I could tell that I was making little impression, and, somewhat frustrated, I blurted out, But this is what the *pope* says; it's what *he* wants." "But," a lady retorted, "The pope doesn't know what it's like to teach catechism to our kids, here in this little town!"

One of the most significant catechetical events of the post-conciliar era was the publication, in 1993, of the *Catechism of the Catholic Church*. This document says of itself that it is addressed primarily to the bishops of the church and is intended to serve as a point of reference in compiling new local catechisms (11). Though it is not suitable for use as a catechetical textbook, the *Catechism* is offered to the church as "a sure and authentic reference text" (Apostolic Constitution *The Deposit of Faith* 4). It provides a comprehensive resource for all catechists who want to deepen their own understanding of Catholic doctrine—and to make sure that what they teach is in keeping with the mind of the church.

When the *Catechism of the Catholic Church* was first issued, some people were disappointed that it did not signal a return to the old cognitive style of learning, complete with the memorization of a series of definitions. In fact, as the *General Directory for Catechesis* would soon show, the church was moving in a totally different direction.

The General Directory for Catechesis

The *General Directory for Catechesis* was published in Rome by the Congregation for the Clergy in 1997. This document will be our guide throughout the rest of this book. It declared catechesis in its various forms to be "a school of faith, an initiation and apprenticeship in the entire Christian life" (30); "it needs to form the personality of the believer" and promote "the trinitarian experience of life in Christ as the center of the life of faith" (33). In addition, catechesis *"must have a catechumenal style, as of integral formation rather than mere information; it must act ... as a means of arousing true conversion"* (29; italics added). This is the reason that the *Directory* insists that the model for all catechesis is the baptismal catechumenate.

The *General Directory for Catechesis* builds on the earlier *General Catechetical Directory* of 1971 but places considerably more emphasis on the function of catechesis as an integral part of evangelization. It states that the two activities are "essential and mutually complementary: go and welcome, proclaim and educate, call and incorporate" (GDC 61). Thus catechesis is seen as a vital aspect of the church's mission to proclaim the Gospel. The parable of the sower (Mk 4:3) is proposed as the inspiration for the whole range of catechetical activity. Just as Jesus proclaimed the Gospel in Palestine two thousand years ago, so today, through the Holy Spirit, he continues "to scatter the word of the Father ever more widely in the field of the world" through the agency of the church. In proclaiming the coming of the kingdom of God, Christ "promises a rich harvest," but "the word of God grows only in a well disposed heart" (15).

Four "fundamental tasks of catechesis" are identified by the *General Directory for Catechesis*: Promoting knowledge of the faith, liturgical education, moral formation, and teaching to pray. These, of course, correspond to the four pillars of the *Catechism*. To them the *Directory* adds education for community life and missionary initiation (85, 86). In the next chapter we shall see how all these tasks are incorporated into the structure of the baptismal catechumenate.

Discussion Questions

For Liturgists and Catechists

- Since "the definitive aim of catechesis" is to lead people into intimate relationship with Christ, what kind of extra-liturgical activities—retreats, days of recollection, presentations on prayer, etc.—could you initiate in your parish that might help in that process?

3. The Baptismal Catechumenate

Discussion Questions

For Catechists

- How do you feel about the insistence of the *General Directory for Catechesis* that the baptismal catechumenate is the model for all catechesis? What changes need to be made in your parish catechetical process in order to conform to this model?

For Liturgists

- Apart from encouraging participation in the rites of the catechumenate, how would it be possible to make your parish community more aware of their role as an initiating community?
- What does it mean to you that at the time of our baptism we are anointed with Christ's offices of priest, prophet, and king? What are the implications of this anointing in terms of your own ministry?

The restoration of the catechumenate (*Constitution on the Sacred Liturgy* 64) has proved to be one of the most dynamic reforms of Vatican II because of the potential growth the process has for both catechumens and the faith community. The Council's *Decree on Missionary Activity in the Church* points out that rather than being "a mere exposition of dogmatic truths and norms of morality," the catechumenate is "a period of formation in the whole Christian life, an apprenticeship of sufficient duration during which the disciples will be joined to Christ their teacher" (14).

The word "apprenticeship" implies that training is gradual, imparting knowledge and understanding of "the way things are done" through inclusion in a group of people already skilled in the field. The apprentice learns both by hands-on instruction and by working alongside, observing, and talking with these "experts." He or she is "inculturated" into the group.

The catechumenate is a sacramental journey by which newcomers to the church are apprenticed in Catholic Christian living and belief, in the midst of the worshiping community that is responsible for their formation. By means of liturgical ritual and symbol, celebrations of the Word, prayer, and exposure to doctrine, the community leads these aspiring Christians to conversion and the development of faith. When they and the catechetical team discern that they are ready to become fully initiated members of the community, they are baptized and confirmed and celebrate first communion.

In 1988, the United States bishops mandated the *Rite of Christian Initiation of Adults*—actually a series of rites within a rite—as the way all adults and children of catechetical age were to be initiated into the Catholic Church. The RCIA includes adaptations for the initiation of children (sometimes mistakenly called the "RCIC"), for people in special circumstances, and for those in danger of death.

The catechumenate consists of four distinct stages:

1. The precatechumenate, or period of initial inquiry.
2. The period of catechumenate itself, during which most of the systematic catechesis is given, accompanied by various rites and celebrations, and the unbaptized begin to live in accordance with Gospel values.
3. Purification and enlightenment, a six-week period of preparation for the initiation sacraments, usually corresponding to the Lenten season.
4. The period of post-baptismal catechesis, or mystagogia, which lasts through the Easter season plus one year.

Perhaps the way the catechumenate "works" is best understood by reflecting on the story of Brenda, an unbaptized lady who was initiated a few years ago in the parish where I was a catechumenate team member.

A woman in her 40s, Brenda had never consciously encountered God until she happened upon some of Andrew Greely's novels. "He made God seem so loving and compassionate," she told our catechumenate team. "I never knew God was like that! I want to learn more."

The Precatechumenate

In the inquiry phase, she shared her own story and listened to those of others in the precatechumenate. She asked basic questions about Christianity and about the church. She heard the great stories of the Hebrew Scriptures—the Exodus, the Covenant, the arrival at the Promised Land—how they prefigured the incarnation and the paschal mystery and how they are played out, in many different ways, in the life of each of us.

When she decided that she wanted to prepare for baptism, we discerned together her readiness to move to the catechumenate. The following Sunday she participated, with other inquirers from the group, in the combined celebration of the rite of acceptance into the order of catechumens and of the rite of welcoming baptized but previously uncatechized adults (RCIA 505–529). The latter group were preparing for confirmation and/or first communion, or reception into the full communion of the Catholic Church. We had not told the inquirers the details of what would take place, so that they might be more deeply impacted by the ritual.

The inquirers gathered with their sponsors and the assembly outside the doors of the church. After greeting them, the presider asked them, "What do you ask of God's Church?" and "What does faith offer you?" They gave short answers, each in his or her own words. Entering the building, the group was welcomed with applause. This was the first time the newcomers had been introduced to the community to which they were being "apprenticed." Each inquirer was accompanied by a sponsor, a companion who would walk him or her throughout the journey to the Easter sacraments.

Sponsors and assembly were asked: "Are you ... ready to help these follow Christ?"

"We are," came the enthusiastic response.

When the inquirers, with their sponsors, were called forward, each was signed on the forehead with the cross, the sign of their "new way of life as catechumens," by the presider; signing of the other senses by the sponsors followed. "Receive the sign of the cross on your ears, / that you may hear the voice of the Lord, ... on your eyes, ... on your lips, ... over your heart, / that Christ may dwell there by faith, ... on your shoulders, / that you may bear the gentle yoke of Christ, ... your hands, ... your feet, / that you may walk in the way of Christ." After the Liturgy of the Word, the new catechumens were called forward again and presented with a Book of the Gospels.

The Catechumenate

Then came the dismissal, which would be repeated each Sunday during their catechumenal formation. The presider explained this ritual to them and to the assembly, and then sent them forth with a catechist to reflect on the lectionary readings. He promised the prayers of the entire community who looked forward "to the day when [they would] share fully in the Lord's Table."

When we reached the room, decorated with liturgical symbols, where we would hold the dismissal catechesis each week, the catechumens shared their impressions of the rite they had just experienced.

"I thought it was beautiful," Brenda said. "It really helped me to understand what this whole thing is about. I'm glad you didn't explain it all to us first. This way helped us to go deeper."

I have described the combined rite of acceptance and welcoming in some detail because it says much about the approach used in the initiation process and about the process itself. It also illustrates the importance of the rites which define the periods of the *Rite of Christian Initiation of Adults*, as well as the minor rituals that are included.

As a catechumen, Brenda began to learn much more about Jesus, as divine and human; about redemption, new life and discipleship—and about God's love. She also discovered many things about herself, as she began to relate the Scriptures and the doctrines of the church to her life experience. We helped her to develop an active prayer life, sharing with her and the rest of the group our own experiences of prayer and introducing them to many different ways of praying.

In the whole extended process of the catechumenate (RCIA 75–117), the sharing and dynamic of the group played a key role. One day, the Sunday's Gospel reading was the parable of the forgiving father, also known as the prodigal son (Lk 15:11–32). The catechist asked questions like, "Which character in the story do you identify with the most? Why do you think this is so? Have you ever had an experience of being badly hurt by someone you loved or trusted? How did you feel? Was it hard to forgive?" After some discussion, she went on, "What about a time when perhaps you did something really hurtful to another person? Did you find it difficult to ask for that persons forgiveness? Have you ever felt angry and resentful because you were passed over for an honor that you felt you deserved? How did you deal with the situation?"

When these topics had been probed through reflection and sharing, the catechist continued: "Notice that the younger son had prepared a little repentance speech in advance. But the father had been watching, hoping that the young man would come home. When he appeared, the old man ran down the road to meet him so that he could hug and kiss him. In the joy of being reunited, the father overlooked the son's misdeeds. Then, look at how gently the father dealt with his resentful older son, who had stayed and worked the farm with him. The father did not regret having celebrated the prodigal's return, but he understood how his other son felt, and reminded him of his love, and concern for that son's welfare. What does all this tell you about God?"

The group discussed these questions for awhile. One man shared how his own teenager had run away from home, how he felt, and his reaction when the boy returned. A woman talked about an experience where she experienced God's forgiveness. Then it was time to move on to the church's teaching on repentance, forgiveness and the sacrament of reconciliation, a doctrine that flowed naturally from the gospel and the group discussion. The catechist added a little anecdote about "going to confession" before Vatican II to help the group understand an aspect of "Catholic culture."

The topic of reconciliation was brought up again, from a different perspective, when the reading told of Jesus' post-resurrection appearance in the upper room and his calling down the Holy Spirit on the apostles, saying, "Whose sins you forgive are forgiven" (Jn 20:23).

As the period of the catechumenate continued, the group was internalizing the content of the sessions and relating their new insights to their own lives. All the while, they were assimilating Christian values and beginning to realize what it would mean to live as a disciple of Jesus Christ.

We could tell that Brenda's conversion was deepening by the personal incidents she shared. "My husband tried to start a fight the other day. But I remembered what Jesus said about love, and about being angry. So I asked for his help, and do you know what? I stayed calm." Or, "There was this gorgeous dress that I wanted in the worst way. But the lady down the street was having a really hard time, so I used the money to help her instead." She paused. "I had to pray real hard about that one!" Soon after she became a catechumen, Brenda began visiting a nursing home regularly with her sponsor, as her part in the mission of the parish community. She was learning the ways of discipleship.

For the unbaptized, it is required that the catechumenate last a minimum of one year. Brenda stayed for two years. She did not feel fully prepared before that to make the total commitment of self that baptism requires; she also needed more time to process all that she had learned and experienced. When Lent arrived for the second time, however, she was ready—eager to share at the eucharistic table and take her part as a full member of the community. The pastor and the catechumenate team agreed with her.

The Rite of Election

On the First Sunday of Lent, Brenda and her sponsor, accompanied by members of her family, went to the cathedral for the celebration of the rite of election of catechumens and of the call to continuing conversion of candidates (RCIA 547–560), which was attended by catechumens and candidates from around the diocese. After the singing, the Scripture readings, and a homily by the bishop, the name of each catechumen was called. "Here I am, Lord," each replied, affirming that it was not the church, but God, that had chosen them for initiation. Brenda's voice was strong and sure.

The bishop asked the sponsors, and then the assembly, if they judged the catechumens ready for the Easter sacraments: "Have they faithfully listened to God's word? ... Have they responded to that word and begun to walk in God's presence? Have they shared the company of their Christian brothers and sisters and joined them in prayer?" To each of these questions, the answer was, "They have." Finally, he addressed the catechumens themselves, asserting that "the Church in the name of Christ ... calls you to the Easter sacraments" and asking, "Do you wish to enter fully into the life of the Church?" The response, "We do," echoed through the cathedral.

The already baptized candidates for full communion were then asked to stand. The bishop asked for testimony from their sponsors, and then exhorted the candidates to "hear the Lord's call to conversion and be faithful to your baptismal covenant."

Purification and Enlightenment

Now began the period of Purification and Enlightenment (RCIA 138–205), when the elect joined the rest of the parish in their Lenten practices, a "spiritual recollection in preparation for the celebration of the paschal mystery." On the Third, Fourth, and Fifth Sundays of Lent, the scrutinies were celebrated. Even during the B and C cycles, the A cycle readings are used each week at the liturgy when the scrutinies are celebrated because the themes of the Gospels—stories of the Samaritan woman, the man born blind, and the raising of Lazarus—correlate with the themes of the scrutinies. These rites are intended for "self-searching and repentance" and are "meant to uncover, then heal all that is weak, defective, or sinful in the hearts of the elect" and to bring out and strengthen what is good. The scrutinies are to be celebrated in such a way "that the faithful in the assembly will also derive benefit" from them (RCIA 141, 145).

After the first scrutiny, the elect are presented with the Creed, to which they will be giving assent at baptism. After the third, a presentation of the Lord's Prayer is made. Traditionally, this prayer is "proper to those who in baptism have received the spirit of adoption," and the elect will recite it with the community when they take part in the eucharistic celebration for the first time.

The Sacraments of Christian Initiation

At last, Easter arrived, and the Vigil was celebrated. Brenda, with the other elect and candidates, joined the assembly for the lighting of the new fire, from which the paschal candle was lit. She walked in procession behind the paschal candle, held high to represent Christ, the light of the world who dispels the darkness of evil and death. She listened to the Scriptures recounting the story of salvation history, culminating in the proclamation of the resurrection itself. After the homily, the litany of the saints was chanted. Then came the rituals of Christian initiation: "Brenda, I baptize you in the name of the Father and of the Son and of the Holy Spirit." "Brenda, be sealed with the Holy Spirit." The whole assembly renewed baptismal promises, then the candidates for full communion made their profession of faith. A little later, it was time to share in the eucharistic meal for the first time. Brenda and her companions were now fully initiated members of the Catholic Christian community.

Fire, water, oil, bread and wine—all are symbols of the new life in Christ, of sharing with him in the paschal mystery, and of the presence of the Holy Spirit. The ancient rituals, dating from the early days of the church, united the newly baptized and the community to those had gone before us through two millennia "signed with the sign of faith."

Mystagogia

When the newly initiated first gathered for the period of mystagogia, we "unpacked" the whole celebration, step by step. It had been, as it always is, a profoundly transcendent and meaningful experience for everyone. They were now beginning to enter into "the mysteries" at a much deeper level than was previously possible.

"It was all so wonderful, so powerful," Brenda declared, "something I'll never forget. I'm so glad you let us find out for ourselves, again, what would happen." Later in the mystagogia period, Brenda was one of those who gave a "testimony talk" at one of the Sunday Masses, sharing with the community what the whole catechumenate experience had meant to her thus far. In this final period, the newly initiated, or neophytes, "experience being fully a part of the Christian community." With the community "they grow in deepening their grasp of the paschal mystery and in making it part of their lives" (RCIA 244).

The story of Brenda, of course, is similar to that of any number of unbaptized people who are initiated into the Catholic Church. With some modifications, and without the baptismal rites, baptized candidates of other faiths, and sometimes Catholics who are uncatechized, follow a similar path.

The Catechumenate
And Contemporary Catechesis

Paragraph 91 of the *General Directory for Catechesis* cites five of the elements of the catechumenate process that "must inspire contemporary catechesis" in all its forms. They are as follows:

1. **The baptismal catechumenate constantly reminds the whole Church of the fundamental importance of the function of initiation and the basic factors which constitute it ....** The pastoral care of Christian initiation is vital for every particular Church. Since the initiation sacraments are the foundation of our whole lives as Christians, carrying with them solemn obligations, it is incumbent upon all of us to reflect upon them frequently. They remind us of the new life of Christ that we share through the waters of baptism. This perspective must be an integral part of all catechesis.

2. **The baptismal catechumenate is the responsibility of the entire Christian community.** It is not just the pastor who initiates new members. "The people of God, as represented by the local Church, should understand and show by their concern that the initiation of adults is the responsibility of all the baptized" (RCIA 9). Engagement with the initiation process will naturally stem from the community's mission to evangelize. Parishioners are particularly urged to welcome newcomers and to interact with them. Later, the community is asked to be present at the various rites of the catechumenate, and to give careful testimony when invited to do so (*ibid*). Initially, responsibility for *all* catechetical programs lies with the parish community. Clearly, the community must also nurture and minister to all those who are involved in those programs, both catechists and participants.

3. **The baptismal catechumenate is also completely permeated by the *mystery of Christ's Passover*. ... The Easter Vigil, focal point of the Christian liturgy, and its spirituality of Baptism inspire all catechesis.** "The whole initiation must bear a markedly paschal character" (RCIA 8). The ceremonies of the Easter Vigil lead us into the very heart of our faith, the paschal mystery. A catechesis modeled on the catechumenate, which by its nature is oriented toward initiation, will naturally keep the Vigil and its triumphant celebration of resurrection in sight during the entire process.

4. **The baptismal catechumenate is also an initial locus of inculturation. ... All catechetical activity participates in this function of incorporating into the catholicity of the Church, authentic "seeds of the word," scattered through nations and individuals.** The interaction between the social and cultural situation in which Jesus lived and his proclamation of the Gospel was the first "'inculturation' of the word of God and is the model of all evangelization by the Church" (GDC 109). While transmitting the Good News, the Church also discerns which elements of the culture are "contrary to the Kingdom of God" and, by the same token, which "riches" of a culture may be incorporated into the church's understanding of the Gospel. Thus, both the church and the culture benefit from the interaction.

5. **The concept of the baptismal catechumenate as *a process of formation and as a true school of the faith* offers post-baptismal catechesis dynamic and particular characteristics.** These are:

   • *Comprehensiveness and integrity of formation.* "A suitable catechesis is provided ... , planned to be gradual and complete in its coverage, accommodated to the liturgical year, and solidly supported by celebrations of the word" (RCIA 75). Paragraph 78 of the RCIA lists the nature of this catechesis: In addition to doctrine itself, it should enlighten faith, direct the heart toward God, foster participation in the liturgy, inspire apostolic activity, and nurture "a life completely in accord with the spirit of Christ." Clearly, this formation corresponds to the "fundamental tasks of catechesis" listed in paragraph 85 of the *General Directory for Catechesis* we discussed in Chapter 2.

   • *Its gradual character expressed in definite stages.* The structure of the baptismal catechumenate, and the significance of each of the stages, have been explained. The schedule, however, is flexible. "The duration of the catechumenate will depend on the grace of God and on various circumstances" (RCIA 76). The Holy Spirit is not

to be coerced or constrained by human schedules!
"The time spent in the catechumenate should be long
enough—several years if necessary—for the conversion
and faith of the catechumens to become strong."
Moreover, the initiation process is but the beginning
of a lifelong journey of conversion.

- *Its connection with meaningful rites, symbols, and
  liturgical signs.* The importance of liturgical rites and
  the part played by Scripture in the journey of faith are
  emphasized in the RCIA. Celebrations and rituals are
  frequently included in the catechetical process. These
  are in addition to the weekly celebrations of the Liturgy
  of the Word, which is the foundation of the
  catechumenal process. Rites and symbolism are
  essential components of the journey of faith, as we shall
  see in Chapter 7.
- *Its constant reference to the Christian community.* The
  catechesis of the RCIA is carried out in the midst of the
  community. This fact ensures that an understanding of
  the community's role is placed in a perspective
  consonant with that expressed in church documents.

As we have seen, besides meeting the needs of those adults
and children of catechetical age who are preparing for baptism,
the *Rite of Christian Initiation of Adults* also includes adaptations for those who are already baptized—people from other
Christian churches and Catholics who have not completed their
initiation. In other words, it provides for post-baptismal catechesis. There is, of course, a fundamental difference in focus between pre-baptismal and post-baptismal catechesis. The latter,
as the *General Directory for Catechesis* (90) notes, "derives
from the sacraments of initiation" which those being catechized
have already received; "'the basis of their conversion is the Baptism which they have already received and whose power they
must develop (RCIA 295).'" This distinction is maintained in the
initiation process.

Those who participate in such a process, from small children
to the elderly, will grow as Christians under the guidance of the

Spirit—as, indeed, do the sponsors and the catechists as they lead each new group through the process. Therefore, "this catechumenal formation should inspire the other forms of catechesis in both their objectives and in their dynamism" (GDC 59).

We have accompanied an adult catechumen on her journey to Easter. In Chapter 5, we will describe a liturgical catechesis session for children that conforms to the catechumenal paradigm. Before doing so, however, an examination of the way faith develops may help us to arrive at a fuller understanding of the catechumenal process.

Discussion Questions

For Liturgists and Catechists

- How can the rites of the catechumenate be planned in such a way that the community is invited to participate as much as possible? Given the architecture and environment of your worship space, in what ways can the meaning of the rites be emphasized?

4. The Formation of Faith

Discussion Questions

For Catechists

- How have you experienced conversion in your own life?
- How does your understanding of conversion and faith development impact your approach to catechesis?

For Liturgists

- How does the liturgical planning in your parish address the particular needs of teenagers and of children? Do you believe that they should be offered liturgical celebrations geared to their respective age groups, or should there be elements of regular parish liturgies that involve and engage them?

In previous chapters, we have been discussing how liturgy and catechesis are intrinsically linked. Now it is time to take a look at the basic sources of all faith formation and how faith itself grows as it is nurtured. Since liturgical catechesis makes extensive use of biblical passages, which are selected to correspond to the seasons of the liturgical year, let us begin with Scripture.

Sacred Scripture

Before Vatican II, Catholics were not exposed to a large portion of the scriptural canon, apart from the very limited selections (two New Testament readings, repeated in a yearly cycle) that were read at Sunday Masses.

Despite papal urging, which began several years before the council opened, Catholics rarely read the Bible privately and Scripture study was almost unknown. It seemed somehow "Protestant" to quote Scripture passages, especially if chapter and verse were included. On the occasions when Catholics did do this, it was usually in the form of "proof texts" to demonstrate the authenticity of a particular doctrine.

However, one of the mandates of the *Constitution on the Sacred Liturgy* was that "the treasures of the Bible are to be opened up more lavishly, so that a richer share in God's word may be provided for the faithful" (51). Accordingly, a new lectionary was prepared, in which a reading from the Hebrew Scriptures and a responsorial psalm were added each Sunday. A three-year lectionary cycle was developed, providing for the reading of almost the entire four Gospels, as well as a large number of passages from both Testaments.

This new lectionary was included in the reformed Roman Missal of Paul VI in 1969. In the apostolic constitution *The Roman Missal*, the pope expressed the hope that the increased number of readings in the lectionary would stimulate a "hunger for the word of God" among all Catholics, so that both "priests and faithful" might prepare themselves more carefully for the liturgical celebration and would daily reflect prayerfully on the Scriptures. "In accord with the teachings of the Second Vatican Council, *all will thus regard the sacred Scripture as the abiding source of spiritual life, the foundation for Christian instruction, and the core of all theological study*" (italics added). In this he was echoing the teaching of the council's *Dogmatic Constitution on Divine Revelation*.

In that document, the council fathers stressed that the church regards revelation as being rooted not only in the Bible but in the Tradition of the church as set forth by the church's teaching office, the Magisterium. "Sacred Tradition and sacred Scripture make up a single sacred deposit of the Word of God, which is entrusted to the Church" (10). Indeed, the two, with the Magisterium, "are so connected and associated that one of them cannot stand without the others."

Sacred Tradition

The word "Tradition"—with a capital "T"—does not have the meaning of a long established custom, belief, or pattern of thought, as is understood in the word written with a small "t." Rather, the *Constitution on Divine Revelation* defines Tradition as "what was handed on by the apostles." It "serves to make the People of God live their lives in holiness and increase their faith." It is the means by which the church passes on through the ages "all that she herself is, all that she believes" (8).

There is, however, "progress" in this Tradition—"a growth in insight into the realities and words that are being passed on." Thus, as the centuries go by, "the Church is always advancing toward the plenitude of divine truth, until eventually the words of God are fulfilled in her." Tradition is built on the lived experience, prayer, ritual, reflection, and daily life of believers, under the guidance of the Holy Spirit.

An inevitable accompaniment of growth is change. While the basic truths of our faith—the Trinity, the paschal mystery, the incarnation, and so on—are unchanging, our understanding and interpretation of them must, of necessity, grow as the church goes forward toward the full realization of the kingdom of God. Doctrine can only be expressed in words, which are inadequate vehicles of mystery. Moreover, over the centuries, word meanings are modified, nuanced, even completely replaced. New words must be found; new ways of expressing meaning come into use. In addition, ongoing discoveries in all fields of learning—technological advances, economic, social and cultural developments—call for the application of Gospel values in new and previously unimagined ways.

The Catechism of the Catholic Church

An expression of the church's doctrine in summary form is contained in the *Catechism of the Catholic Church*, "an official text of the Church's Magisterium, which authoritatively gathers ... the events and fundamental salvific truths which express the faith common to the People of God and which constitute the indispensable basic reference for catechesis" (*General Directory for Catechesis* 124). However, the fact that the body of doctrine is living and growing is illustrated by the fact that the definitive Latin version, published in 1997 and issued in the English translation in 2000, differs significantly from the 1993 edition, notably in the expanded, more clearly defined teaching on the use of the death penalty (*Catechism* 2266). As time goes on, we may doubtless expect other modifications to the document.

"The axis of the *Catechism of the Catholic Church* is Jesus Christ," and "it is oriented in two directions: toward God and toward the human person." The work is structured around the mystery of the Trinity. "The mystery of the human person is presented throughout" and contemplated in the light of the humanity of Jesus, the perfect man" (GDC 123). The *Directory* suggests that the doctrine of the *Catechism* "can be distilled into the following remark of the Council: 'Jesus Christ, by revealing the mystery of the Father and of his love, fully reveals man to himself [sic] and brings to light his most high calling' (*Pastoral Constitution on the Church in the Modern World* 22a)" (GDC 123).

Paragraph 11 of the *Catechism* explains that its aim is to present "an organic synthesis of the essential and fundamental contents of Catholic doctrine, as regards both faith and morals." Thus, it is an invaluable resource, and every catechist will benefit from consulting it before a catechetical session, in reference to the particular doctrine to be taught.

The General Directory for Catechesis

The *Catechism* is "a statement of the Church's faith and of catholic doctrine, attested to or illumined by Sacred Scripture, the Apostolic Tradition, and the Church's Magisterium (Apostolic Constitution *The Deposit of Faith* 3). The *General Directory for Catechesis* "provides the basic principles of pastoral theology taken from the Magisterium of the Church, and in a special way from the Second Vatican Council (*General Catechetical Directory* [1971] Introduction)" (GDC 120). The CCC and the GDC are "mutually complementary." The first "is an act of the Magisterium of the Pope," and the second "carries that authority normally vested by the Holy See in instruments of orientation by approving them and confirming them." As such, the *General Directory for Catechesis* is "an official aid for the transmission of the Gospel message and for the whole of catechetical activity." In other words, the *Catechism* contains the content of the faith, while the *Directory* lays down the manner in which the content of faith is to be communicated.

Neither the teaching of the *Catechism* nor the Scripture alone is sufficient for a complete catechesis. Together, however, according to the *General Directory for Catechesis*, they form the "two basic sources of inspiration for all catechetical activity in our time. Sacred Scripture, as 'the word of God written under the inspiration of the Holy Spirit' (*Constitution on Divine Revelation* 9), and the *Catechism of the Catholic Church* ... are called, each in its own way and according to its specific authority, to nourish catechesis in the Church of today" (128). By using the lectionary readings as the focus of weekly catechetical sessions, and developing from them a teaching on a particular doctrine, the liturgical catechesis integrates the use of both sources.

Faith

Since its function is to act as a guide for catechesis, the *General Directory for Catechesis* often uses the word "faith" to refer to content—what the Catholic Church believes and teaches. But faith can also be defined in relational terms, as our response to an invitation to intimacy. "At every time and in every place," God draws close and from the moment of his or her coming into being, calls each person into communion with the persons of the Trinity (CCC 1). "The desire for God is written in the human heart." Because every person has been created and is held in existence by love, each must freely acknowledge that love and entrust himself or herself to God (see CCC 27).

God's communication with us through the centuries is known as revelation. But this is not something static, a series of truths gradually made known to humanity to give us a basis for belief. Rather, it is God's *self*-revelation. It came first through the prophets and the events recorded in the First Testament, and eventually in the Second Person, the Word, who became incarnate in Jesus Christ. Faith, the *Catechism of the Catholic Church* affirms, is our response to this revelation. In responding and opening ourselves to God, we are given "a superabundant light" to assist us in our search for the "ultimate meaning of … life" (26). Obviously, in order for our faith to grow and bear fruit, we must first come to know, on a personal level, the God who is revealed to us in Jesus Christ. It is not enough merely to read and be taught about God.

The seed of faith is sown in the soil of our minds and hearts. It is the gift by which we come to trust God more and more fully, deepening our relationship as we accept the validity of God's loving communication. The soil must be tilled, the seed cherished and nurtured.

Let us look for a moment at the way human relationships are formed and apply those principles to the communion and intimacy with Jesus Christ that catechesis aims to mediate in every person. Obviously, a prerequisite of any relationship is a personal encounter between the people involved, so that they may get to know one another. The better we know them, the clearer the meaning of their actions becomes (see GDC 100).

"Even in the human order the love which one person has for another causes that person to wish to know the other all the more" (85). As a relationship with God grows and deepens, a more comprehensive type of catechesis will eventually be sought, with an explanation of God's whole plan of salvation.

Catechesis approached from a personal and relational perspective will avoid the pitfall of presenting abstract doctrinal concepts, unrelated to the experience of God in daily living—or, as someone put it, "answering questions that have not been asked and introducing topics that are irrelevant in a particular life at a particular time." Thus, at all stages of catechesis, human experience must play an important part, showing "how the Gospel fully satisfies the human heart" and "how the great themes of faith … are always sources of light and life for the human being" (117). The spirit of the Beatitudes "must permeate" the teaching of morality and the Ten Commandments, rooting them in the virtues present in the heart of every person. Catechesis on the liturgy itself "shall make constant reference to the great human experiences represented by the signs and symbols of liturgical actions."

Having firmly established a relationship with Jesus Christ, the person being catechized eventually comes to the point of giving *"free assent to the whole truth that God has revealed"* (CCC 150). In the case of the catechumen, this assent is ratified at the time of baptism during the Easter Vigil. For all of us, this same assent is repeated each Sunday in the Creed.

Faith, then, can mean the content of belief. It can also be understood as a response, a total commitment in loving trust, to God's self-revelation. At the same time, a mature faith includes believing, with both head and heart, in all that has been revealed by God in Scripture and in the Tradition of the church.

The *General Directory for Catechesis* develops a similar understanding of faith and conversion. "Faith is a personal encounter with Jesus Christ, making of oneself a disciple of him. This demands a permanent commitment to think like him, to judge like him and to live as he lived (cf. *Catechesi Tradendae* 20b)" (53). It is a "Yes" to Jesus Christ, expressed as "a trustful abandonment to God and a loving assent" to revelation. "This is possible only by means of the action of the Holy Spirit (cf. CCC 150 and 176)" (54). Faith, the *Directory* continues, "involves a change of life ... a profound transformation of mind and heart ... [that] manifests itself at all levels of the Christians existence. ... Faith and conversion arise from the '*heart,*' that is, they arise from the depth of the human person," involving all that that person is (55).

The Development of Faith

In GDC paragraph 56, four "important moments" in the process of faith development and conversion are noted:

1. *Interest in the Gospel.*
2. *Conversion,* when the "first moment of interest ... requires a period of searching (cf. RCIA 6 and 7)" so that it is transformed into a firm and mature "fundamental option (cf. *Ad Gentes* 13; *Evangelii Nuntiandi* 10; *Redemptoris Missio* 46; *Veritatis Splendor* 66; RCIA 10)." In other words, the choice to become a disciple of Christ must be a free, considered, and informed decision.
3. *Profession of faith.* Through catechesis, believers are initiated "in knowledge of faith and apprenticeship in the Christian life." This promotes a spiritual journey that "brings about a 'progressive change in outlook and morals' (*Decree on Missionary Activity in the Church* 13b)." The new disciple "is then ready to make an explicit, living and fruitful profession of faith."
4. *Journeying towards perfection.* "The profession of baptismal faith is but the foundation of a spiritual building which is destined to grow. The baptized ... seeks to realize the desire of Christ: 'Be perfect as your heavenly Father is perfect' (Mt 5:48)."

If we refer back to Chapter 3, it is clear that the stages and gradual formation of the catechumenal process correspond to these stages of conversion.

In applying the understanding of faith development outlined above, the *General Directory for Catechesis* shows a deep sensitivity to the needs of various age groups. Of small children, whose cognitive faculties are not yet strongly developed, the *Directory* states: "The catechesis of children is necessarily linked with their life situation and conditions. ... Infancy and childhood ... must ... be understood as a decisive moment for subsequent stages of faith." The catechetical process "seeks to develop ... a sense of trust, of freedom, of self-giving, of invocation and of joyful participation. Central aspects of the formation of children are training in prayer and introduction to Sacred Scripture (cf. Sacred Congregation for Divine Worship, *Directory for Masses with Children*; AAS 66 (1974) pp. 30–46)" (178). The gradual nature of the formation provided to youngsters in the baptismal catechumenate suggests that there is plenty of time for more detailed explanations of church teaching when the children are older. They must first get to know who Jesus is and enjoy a loving relationship with him so they can begin to live as his disciples.

Catechesis for teenagers, GDC 185 states, "should be proposed in new ways which are open to the sensibilities and problems of this age group." All of us who have worked with young people know that to hold their attention it is necessary to approach them "where they are"—to deal with topics which they perceive to have immediate importance for their lives and to be non-judgmental in discussing their actions and ideas. At the same time, it is necessary to propose to them Christian perspectives and solutions to problems. "A necessary 'adaptation of catechesis to young people' is urged, in order to translate into their terms 'the message of Jesus with patience and wisdom and without betrayal' (*On Catechesis in Our Time* 40)."

Even when dealing with adults, adaptations must be made to meet a variety of situations and contexts. People with disabilities ("persons particularly beloved of the Lord"), people who for many reasons are marginalized, professionals with special training, and those living either in rural settings or in cities—all of these need different approaches sensitive to their life experiences (GDC 189–192).

Catechists who minister in specialized and sometimes difficult situations such as these must be helped and supported by the Christian community. So, too, must those who work in a regular parish setting. All of them are seeking to help people to grow in faith: to put them into intimacy with Jesus Christ, to transmit faithfully the Gospel message, and to form them in discipleship so they may live the life of grace.

Discussion Question

For Liturgists and Catechists

- *The Constitution on the Sacred Liturgy* states that renewal of the liturgy is contingent on promoting "warm and living love" (24) for sacred Scripture. What steps are being taken in your parish to increase love and understanding of the Scriptures?

5. A Lectionary-Based Session

Discussion Questions

For Catechists

- What changes might you have to make in the methodology you are using and in the approach to catechesis in your parish in order to offer catechetical formation, modeled on the catechumenate, to all age groups?
- As a catechist, how do you feel about sharing aspects of your own faith journey during a catechetical session? Do you find it difficult to talk about your own relationship with God?

For Liturgists

- How do you see your role as a liturgist in relation to the process of liturgical catechesis? Are there any ways in which you can facilitate that process?

From our discussion so far, it seems that the *General Directory for Catechesis* is calling for a radical change in the way many of us approach catechesis. We may have to "unlearn" many of our basic assumptions and revise the methodology we have been using in religious education classrooms for years!

It is often very difficult to give up the understanding of catechesis as primarily imparting knowledge of dogma, and replace that understanding with Pope John Paul's insistence that establishing a relationship with Jesus is of primary importance. It is hard to remember that our goal is to form disciples and that "promoting knowledge of the faith," though important, is only one of the six fundamental tasks of catechesis cited by the *General Directory for Catechesis* (85). It takes time, prayer, reflection, openness to change and growth, and a study of the catechumenal model on which the new directive is based.

One way in which this model can be implemented is to adopt a liturgical or lectionary-based approach to catechesis. What does a typical session of liturgical catechesis "look like"—and how, in practical terms, does it differ from a religion class that follows the school model?

Environment

The first difference is in the environment, the location where the meeting is held. It is desirable that this is *not* a classroom but a more informal space where participants can sit in a circle rather than in rows of desks.

The room is suitably decorated with banners, pictures, symbolic objects, perhaps plants or flowers, and other expressions of the liturgical season or the Sunday readings. Sometimes the group themselves may be asked to bring symbols that will be added to those already in place. A cloth in the appropriate liturgical color covers the stand or table where the Bible or Lectionary will be placed with a large candle beside it. If possible, an area of the room is set aside as a "prayer corner."

Before the session is described, it should be noted that the lectionary readings that will be "broken open" are those for the *upcoming* Sunday. In this way all who participate in the catechetical sessions will be better prepared to listen to and have dialogue with the readings that will be proclaimed at the liturgy. This, of course, is different from the practice of the catechumenate, where catechumens, unable to share fully in the Liturgy of the Eucharist, are dismissed after the homily to reflect on the readings they have just heard.

Beginning the Session

When the group arrives, the catechist greets each person warmly and personally. For large groups or children who do not know one another well, an ice-breaker or community builder might be helpful in the first few sessions so that participants may start to form community. While the group dynamic is of great importance in the formation process, it is often difficult to share feelings and experiences in a gathering of semi-strangers. A certain level of trust and familiarity needs to be developed. (Note: If the group is large—10 to 15 is an ideal number—it may be necessary to break up into smaller groups for some of the discussion.)

The next two pages contain a reproduction of a session plan for the feast of the Baptism of the Lord, Cycle B, from the *Celebrating the Lectionary* materials published by Resource Publications, Inc. It is intended for intermediate-age children (between 9 and 11). Sessions for other age groups will differ to varying degrees, but the basic structure will remain the same.

Opening the Session

The session opens and closes with a prayer experience related to the theme(s) to be explored that day. It is usually helpful to include a song, hymn, or psalm; singing together is another way to build community. In Chapter 7, some suggestions for praying with groups and individuals are presented.

Introducing the Theme

It may be helpful to begin the session process by asking, "How have you noticed God working in your life this week? Can you think of an example?" The ensuing discussion will need to be brief, but it may set the tone for the whole session and will focus the participants attention.

Our model session design introduces the theme by inviting the children to search for signs of God's presence that are hid-

Unit 3: In the Fullness of Time	**January 9, 2000**
Week 7: God Is Pleased	**Baptism of the Lord**

OPENING

Welcome the group. Spend some time talking about the highlights of the week. When everyone has gathered, take attendance and acknowledge birthdays. Ask all those who brought a baptism remembrance to place it on the prayer table. Ask someone to light the Christ candle. Pray together from the newsprint.

> +Loving God, people have always wondered about you;
> they have longed for signs from you.
> Help us feel your presence today.
> Help us know deep inside ourselves that you are always with us
> for ever and ever. Amen.

Sing or listen to: "I Will Sing, I Will Sing" from *Rainbow Sing-along* or "A Song of Praise" from *God Is...*

Morning/Evening Prayer Option: For evening prayer, light a candle. Sing the Morning or Evening hymn, then sing Psalm 67 or Psalm 132 from *Singing Morning and Evening Prayer.*

INTRODUCING THE THEME

Tell the group that hidden in the meeting area are ten signs of God's presence. Invite them to find the hidden signs. When all have been recovered, ask the following questions.

- **Why are these signs of God's presence?**
- **What other signs can you think of?**
  (e.g., in the church, in your home, in the community, in the world)

EXPLORING THE THEME

Explain that signs are like clues that help us piece together a mystery. Before hearing the Scripture for this week, suggest that the group use some clues to discover who the main character in the reading will be. Pass around the bag of Mystery Clues you prepared in advance. Ask everyone to take one slip until all the slips are gone. Ask someone to begin by saying, "This character...," and then reading his or her clue. Invite the others to try to guess who the "character" is. Repeat with each clue until the group has guessed that it is the Holy Spirit. Have the remaining clues read aloud.

- **Which of the clues describes best what you think and know about the Holy Spirit?** *(Talk about what they have learned in the past, recalling any stories.)*

We are going to listen to this week's Gospel as a pre-recorded reading on tape. Please get comfortable where you are and close your eyes. Listen and imagine you are one of the people right there hearing and seeing John the Baptist and Jesus. Remember that the story takes place before Jesus is well known. It is our first encounter with Jesus since he was an adolescent "lost" in the Temple. He has not yet started teaching or healing people. *(If possible, dim the lights in the meeting area. Then play the recording of Mark 1:7–11. Turn off the tape recorder. Invite everyone to open their eyes when they are ready.)*

- **What do you think it would be like to have an experience like the one described?** *(e.g., scary, exciting, confusing, rewarding, affirming, embarrassing)* **Why?**

Encourage group members to talk about how they think Jesus would have felt and reacted with the heavens opening, the voice coming, and hearing the loving words. Note to the group that Mark does not record who heard the voice or saw what Jesus saw.

- **What questions do you think Jesus might have wanted to ask the Spirit?**

Hand out the Bibles and ask everyone to turn to Mark 1:7–11.

On the recording, we only heard one voice. **Read the passage to yourselves and identify other voices and sounds that might have been part of the experience** *(e.g., John's preaching, people calling out to each other, water lapping and splashing, children playing, Jesus and John speaking, wind as the Spirit came, the voice.)* **Let's make our own recording of this passage with all these sounds.** *(Help group members get organized among themselves, working cooperatively and taking turns. Make more than one recording if it is helpful to give everyone a chance to have the part they want. Afterward, talk about the experience.)*

Young and old, we are God's sons and daughters, and the Holy Spirit is in our lives. Imagine people today feeling deep inside a voice saying to them, "You are my own dear child. I am pleased with you."

- **Who do you think might hear this voice?**
- **Who in your life or in the world do you think longs to hear these words?** *(Ask them to name people and why they selected that person.)*
- **Would you like to hear these words spoken to you? Have you heard them as a result of your baptism? What experiences have you had that tell you God loves you?**

Share stories of any experiences you may have had of God's being pleased with you.

INTEGRATING THE THEME

Option A: **Visual Images.** Using the craft supplies provided, ask the youth to create a 3-D image, abstract or realistic, of this week's story or their experience of it.

Option B: **Reminders of the Spirit.** Invite the youth to make bookmarks to remind people that God's Spirit is with them. On the bookmarks, suggest they write phrases like: "You are God's child, and God is pleased with you," or "Rejoice! The Spirit is with you," or "May God's Spirit be with you today and always." When you've finished writing the words, decorate the bookmarks with the markers. Scatter the bookmarks in music issues throughout the church as a happy surprise for others.

Option C: **Jesus' Baptism/Our Baptism.** Distribute copies of the Activity Sheet and pens. Give the group time to complete the sheet. Share responses and any additional information the youth may have about the images, symbols, etc. *Answers:* 1. Shell, dove, candle. 2. John, God, John, Isaiah. *Crossword Answers:* Down: Jerusalem, Messenger, untie, baptized, prophets, turn. Across: Jordan, desert, spirit, people, forgive, Mark, straight.

CLOSING

Gather around the prayer table. Relight the Christ candle. Look again at the remembrances of baptism that the youth placed on the table. Review with them the baptism ritual from the Activity Sheet, "Baptism Review." Then invite the group to renew their baptismal vows after you. (Use the copy of the vows that you have brought.) After the renewal of baptismal vows you may wish to bless each child on the head, saying:

"You, *(name)*, are God's beloved child, and God is well pleased with you."

Sing or listen to: "Jesus Came" from *Rainbow Sing-along* or "Happy Are You" from *God of My Life*

Morning/Evening Prayer Option: Close with the appropriate Canticle, Intercessions, and Our Father from *Singing Morning and Evening Prayer.*

den in the room and then discuss them. Some of the items suggested on the accompanying catechist resource sheet are water, a leaf, a cross, a picture of a baby, and a mirror (the last one is of great importance). A variety of other age-appropriate activities related to the theme of the day may be used for this segment of the session. Occasionally, an appropriate story may be used. All activities should be followed by open-ended questions that connect the theme to the children's own life experiences.

The *Celebrating the Lectionary* design for this particular Sunday continues with a guessing game related to the Holy Spirit, using a provided activity sheet. This leads into a pre-recorded reading of the Gospel for the week. Some weeks, the first or second reading is used instead of, or in conjunction with, the Gospel. A few other ways that the readings may be introduced are: proclamation (by the catechist or by a good reader in the group); dramatization, if a story is involved; storytelling, if the catechist happens to be a good storyteller (perhaps embellishing the peripheral details a little to add interest); and guided imagery meditation, leading to personal reflection and prayer. If the story (from the Hebrew Scriptures or the Gospels) is very well known, another story on the same theme may be told and then related to the Gospel itself, especially if the group is composed of older children, teens or adults.

Expanding the Theme

Much as in the example of the catechumenate we considered in Chapter 3, the theme is now explored by means of a discussion, again introduced by meaningful questions. (This is when the catechist really becomes a facilitator, sensitive to the circumstances and feelings of the participants, as well as the group dynamics.) The objective of the questions is to invite the participants (children in this case) to explore the themes of the readings in relation to their own lives and share their insights with the group. It is important that the questions be open-ended and that an "expected" answer is not implied.

In this connection, an incident that occurred years ago comes to mind. I was teaching a class of third-graders in a Catholic school with the topic of "God's Gifts." I had approached the question in a fairly impersonal way. I asked, "Can you think of some of the gifts God has given us?" rather than "What are some of the gifts and talents God has given *you*?" or, "How do you feel about them?" After hearing the usual list of blessings received—home, family, food, pets, being artistic, Jesus, friends—I asked, "Why has God given us all these things?" Back came the reply from the whole class in that sing-song way children have of reciting well-learned facts in unison: "Because-he-*loves*-us."

Obviously the question had not engaged them on a deep, personal level. They had not internalized an understanding of their gifts and talents as expressions of God's overwhelming love for each of them. The incident remains in my memory because at the time I felt that a great opportunity had been missed. Somehow I had failed that whole year to really convey God's amazing and unconditional love to them. But it was not until I began working in a catechumenal setting that I understood the reason this had happened. Both the preceding lessons and the questions themselves had failed *because I was trying to teach them in an abstract way* rather than to impact them on the level of a personal relationship with God.

So the questions asked must always relate to the participant's personal experience: What in your own life does this reading bring to mind? What happened? How did you feel? What did you do? Can you see how God was active in your life at that time? Can you see the event differently now from when it first happened? The whole questioning-reflecting-sharing process will, of course, vary according to the age and maturity of the group.

After the questions, an activity is introduced for the purpose of extending the exploration of the theme. In our example, it is a further examination of the reading itself, followed by more discussion and sharing. However, there are many alternatives: a creative writing exercise, an art or craft activity, a reflection and discussion exercise, a word puzzle, acting out or miming an incident, to name a few. This activity seeks to help participants enter more deeply into the theme, internalize it, and understand its implications for daily Christian living.

Introducing Doctrine

When the "Expanding" phase of the session is completed, it is a good time to consider the doctrinal component. *Celebrating the Lectionary* includes a background sheet that suggests what aspect of Catholic teaching flows from the Scripture readings and references the appropriate paragraphs from the *Catechism of the Catholic Church*. Those using alternative materials may want to use a book entitled *Lectionary Index for the Catechism of the Catholic Church*, which correlates the lectionary readings with the *Catechism* (McBrien).

Many times, the session material introduces and discusses the particular doctrine sufficiently so that children will be able to understand and internalize it. Only a few words may be needed to focus on and re-emphasize the topic. However, it is always a good idea for the catechist to become familiar with the paragraphs concerned by consulting the *Catechism*. If time permits, other writings may provide additional valuable resources: Scripture commentaries, the works of other catechists and theologians, as well as liturgical texts and other official church documents. Use of such resources will, of course, be more necessary in preparing to catechize teens and adults rather than the children.

In the session we are considering, on the theme of the Baptism of the Lord, the following doctrinal connections are suggested: the historical fact that Jesus, the one without sin, was ritually cleansed of sin by John; Jesus makes possible baptism in the Spirit, which differs from the baptism of John; through his resurrection, Jesus transformed a Jewish bathing ritual into a universal sign of salvation; Christian baptism incorporates us into the people of God, the Body of Christ, sealing us with the Holy Spirit; baptism grants us certain rights and holds us accountable for responsibilities. *Catechism* references are given for each of these concepts. The catechist has a good deal of choice here and must decide which of the approaches to select by referring back to the group discussion and the activities chosen for the session.

Surely, someone may say, this is a rather haphazard method of teaching doctrine. How can we be certain that there is enough content and that it is taught "systematically," as the documents require?

The National Catechetical Directory, *Sharing the Light of Faith*, includes a list of the Catholic faith's basic beliefs with which everyone should be familiar:

- **The Mystery of the One God**: Trinity Sunday, Baptism of the Lord, and Pentecost
- **Creation**: Lent, Easter
- **Jesus Christ**: All Sundays, especially Christ the King, Epiphany, Baptism, Palm Sunday, Presentation, and Advent Sundays
- **The Holy Spirit**: Sundays of Easter, Pentecost, Baptism of the Lord
- **The Church**: Easter season
- **The Sacraments**: Baptism of the Lord, Lent, Easter season
- **The Life of Grace**: Lent-Easter
- **The Moral Life**: Ordinary Time (and throughout the CTL program)
- **Mary and the Saints**: Advent, All Saints', Marian feasts, and some Sundays of Ordinary Time
- **Death, Judgment, and Eternity**: End of Ordinary Time, Advent, All Saints'

It may surprise some readers to discover that all of these basic beliefs are addressed in the lectionary readings *every year*! As we return to them again and again, we will be able to benefit from the evangelists' differing perspectives, thereby deepening understanding. They will become an integral part of each person's life of faith.

Integrating the Theme

The session closes with another activity, exercise, or discussion designed to concretize the day's learnings in terms of the living out of the paschal mystery. *Celebrating the Lectionary* calls it "Integrating the Theme," and our session model includes three options: two craft projects and a written activity.

Suggestions for living the day's theme may be made at this time, particularly those relating to ministry to others. During the whole of his pontificate, John Paul II has labored to impress upon the world the need to work for peace, social justice, and, in the last few years, for environmental protection. We catechists will want to include references to these needs in our weekly sessions if the material we are using does not do so. When possible, opportunities should be offered for those we are catechizing to put their learning into practice.

Catechist Preparation

The necessity for the catechist to be personally prepared must be emphasized. Preparation for a lectionary-based session is not quite the same as that for teaching a class where a religious education text is used. It involves careful, prayerful reading, in terms of the catechist's own life and of the Scriptures that will be "broken open," so that understanding will not be just intellectual but from the heart. During the session itself, it is often helpful if the catechist shares his or her own experience relating to the reading. Deciding which way this is to be done may require some preparation. This is in addition to the usual planning for the session and the assembling of all necessary materials.

Benefits of Lectionary-Based Catechesis

Having looked briefly at the design and structure of lectionary-based catechesis, let us finally examine the benefits of using this paradigm in a parish setting.

As we have noted, the *General Directory for Catechesis* deplores the fact that today's catechetical practices often have a "weak and fragmentary link with the liturgy" (30). They give little attention to the liturgical year or to ritual and symbol. Yet Pope John Paul II emphasizes that "catechesis is intrinsically linked with the whole of liturgical and sacramental activity" (*On Catechesis in Our Time* 23). A catechesis modeled on the catechumenate, in accordance with the *General Directory for Catechesis*, uses the liturgy itself as its primary text and employs the lectionary readings as the principal resource for weekly sessions. Like the catechumenate itself, this moves the whole process into the context of the living prayer of the community, tying it closely to the liturgy and the unfolding seasons of the liturgical year. With the rest of the weekly assembly, participants are involved in a journey with Christ through his life, death and resurrection. Of course, the degree to which the community celebration is vibrant and participatory significantly affects the extent to which individuals are enabled to enter deeply into the mysteries being celebrated.

The Liturgy of the Word is a "dialogue" between God and God's people, "taking place through the Holy Spirit" (*Introduction to the Lectionary* 28). With the Liturgy of the Eucharist, it forms a single act of worship. Through the readings and the homily, the paschal mystery is proclaimed, and it actually becomes present in the Liturgy of the Eucharist (see *Constitution on the Sacred Liturgy* 6, 47). Thus, more familiarity and reflection on the Word will lead to a deeper level of involvement in the whole eucharistic celebration.

In preparation for the "full, conscious and active participation" in the liturgy called for in the *Constitution on the Sacred Liturgy* (14), we are urged in various documents to read and reflect on the assigned Scripture passages before each Mass. A catechesis that develops and guides such reflection helps us to be more aware of the Lord speaking to us and listen more intently when the Word is proclaimed. We ask, "What response does the Scripture call forth from me as an individual, and from us as a community?" Instead of a time for daydreaming, the Liturgy of the Word becomes an opportunity to dialogue with Jesus. Relationships with him will be deepened, and lives will be more conformed to Gospel values. At the same time, the opportunity is offered to develop a greater knowledge and love for Scripture, so it may be used both as an aid to prayer and a guide to life.

A lectionary-based, liturgical catechesis provides a very solid, comprehensive formation for Christian living. The catechumenate is a process of *initiation* which helps unbaptized catechumens begin to form a relationship with Jesus, and baptized candidates to deepen their relationship with him. Through this relationship, they may become disciples, living by Gospel values. The process, then, is a beginning, and an apprenticeship. It is not intended to be sufficient for a lifetime. The conversion and growth process does not suddenly end with the Easter Vigil and the mystagogy, as our religious education used to end when we had completed all our courses. Initiation is just the beginning. *On Catechesis in Our Time* stresses that "for catechesis to be effective, it must be permanent, and *it would be quite useless* if it stopped short at the threshold of maturity, since catechesis ... proves no less necessary for adults" (43; italics added).

Those who have been baptized but not fully catechized are in need of a catechumenal type of formation, whether they be children, youth, young adults or elderly. *After* this period of apprenticeship in the Christian life (whenever that may be for each individual), they will expand their knowledge and understanding. But they will already have the formation which will help them to benefit from this knowledge. Their lives will be centered on the liturgy. As disciples of Jesus they will be participating in the community's mission, sharing prayer and Scripture as they enter more and more deeply into mystery. Through gradual, consistent exposure to the public prayer of the Church and the weekly Liturgy of the Word, they will encounter all the basic truths of Catholic belief and internalize them. Then it will be time to examine them in greater detail. So for adults and older teens who are already catechized, their weekly dialogue with the Scriptures will be supplemented by a more cognitive approach to Catholic doctrine.

From a more administrative standpoint, liturgical catechesis for children and teens is tied neither to a curriculum nor to the school year. There is no sense of having to "finish the book," nor of graduating from religious education in the eighth or the twelfth grades. There is no expectation that all seven- to eight-year-olds will automatically be ready to celebrate the sacraments of penance and first communion on the particular dates scheduled by the parish. The process is not geared to grades or age level. The cycle of the liturgical year continues all through life, and, in the well-developed eucharistic community, the journey of faith continues with it.

When the catechesis of children is removed from the restrictions of a curriculum (which may have very little connection with the scriptural and prayer themes that inform the Sunday liturgies) and is situated in the heart of the worshiping community, that community is able to fulfill its responsibility to evangelize. Thus, the community models and nurtures the faith of its children as it does that of newcomers in the catechumenate. Catechetical sessions and liturgical involvement (including participating in mission after the dismissal) complement each other in the faith formation of children. They are drawn powerfully into mystery by participating in the symbolic rituals of the eucharistic celebration. The assembly will benefit from the presence of the children and will be challenged to ongoing conversion by the witness they are called upon to offer.

The bonds of the community are also strengthened by the fact that all age groups, including the adults, have listened to and dialogued with the same readings. In this way, family conversation on the message of the Gospel is encouraged and each family member grows together in the journey of faith.

Discussion Questions

For Liturgists and Catechists

- What are some possible ways in which the themes of the weekly readings can be made to "come alive" for participants in the catechetical process?

6. Rites, Signs, And Symbols

Discussion Questions

For Catechists

- The function of symbolic rites is to lead us into mystery. Do you provide experiences that will help those you catechize to more deeply appreciate the power and symbol, and to gain new insights into the themes of your catechetical sessions?

For Liturgists

- Given that many people are unaware of the importance and function of symbols in liturgical worship, what are some of the ways you can help your assembly to a deeper appreciation of the symbolic?

Symbol and ritual are at the very heart of liturgical celebration. Therefore, they must play a vital part in liturgical catechesis. We have seen how the catechumenate makes use of rites during the whole initiation process to help catechumens and candidates gain new insights into the reality of life in Christ. It is important, therefore, to understand their significance and their role in Catholic worship.

Signs and Symbols

Symbolic rituals, great and small, are part of the fabric of human life. They are used everywhere by people who gather—to celebrate, to mourn, to rejoice, to mark important events, or even to conduct routine business. Examples of commonly used symbolic actions are the pledge of allegiance, an opening prayer, the introduction of a speaker or performer. More specific rituals surround the swearing-in of a president, a high school or college graduation, initiation into an organization, or the celebration of a marriage.

A country's flag, hoisted above a tall building, carried at an international sports event, or flying from the mast of a naval ship, evokes feelings of pride and patriotism. It calls to mind, though not explicitly, great events in the nations history: military and moral victories, courage in adversity, and the principles for which that country stands. This is the power of symbols; they suggest events and inner realities beyond immediate sense perception.

Sacramentality and Sacraments

In everyday speech, the terms "sign" and "symbol" are used interchangeably. But in terms of religious experience, some differentiation must be made. A sign is understood as designating or pointing to something (as in the way a road sign points in the direction of a given location). A religious symbol, on the other hand, engages not only our mind but our emotions and deepest faith perceptions. It leads us beyond what we see, hear, or experience to an encounter with God at a profound level, mediating realities that cannot be expressed in words and making them present. It leads us into mystery.

Everywhere in creation, signs "point to" God's presence. God speaks to us in "light and darkness, wind and fire, water and earth, the tree and its fruit" (*Catechism of the Catholic Church* 1147). Creation, then, can be said to be "sacramental." The church expresses this universal sacramentality in a ritual way with the seven canonical sacraments, which are celebrated within the community of believers. The symbols lead us beyond the perceptions of our senses into mystery. Through the Holy Spirit, we are led to an authentic encounter with Christ, who graces us in unique ways throughout our lives and continually feeds us with the bread of life.

Religious rites may be regarded as bridges linking people with God, who is the Holy Mystery and the Wholly Other. Since we are both body and spirit, we need to use our physical senses to receive and communicate spiritual meaning. The symbols used in liturgical rituals illustrate this need. They consist of commonplace things that are used universally by humans and speak to us at the most basic level of life: hope and renewal, food and drink. Things "given by the earth" (water, bread, oil, wine), words (the readings, the prayers recited), and gestures (the sign of the cross, hands extended in blessing) mediate spiritual realities. It should be noted that language itself is symbolic and a vehicle for communicating thoughts and ideas in concrete form. Like the other sacramental symbols, words are sacramental signs and instruments of God's presence with us. Through them, we are able to make real (real-ize) meanings that would otherwise elude us. But we can never fully plumb the depths of their reality; we sense that there is always something more, beyond what we apprehend. This is the meaning of mystery.

We see the use of symbolic ritual throughout the Scriptures. The Ark of the Covenant, for example, signifies God's continued presence with Israel, and the Passover supper symbolizes a reliving of the events of the Exodus. Bread and wine, signifying life-sustaining food and drink, were used by Christ himself as vehicles of his self-gift in the paschal mystery. In social communication, humans need language and actions to convey thoughts and experiences to others.

The Eucharistic Liturgy

The eucharistic liturgy has its origins in the Jewish experience of Passover, an event still called to mind each year in the seder supper. In this celebration, participants enter into the Exodus event and experience its liberation as present now, transcending time and space. In the same way, Catholics believe that the paschal mystery is made present to us through liturgical rites and symbols, which have their origin in the Christian experience of Christ's death and resurrection.

The liturgy has a basic order and structure that makes up one composite act of prayer, in which all present are participants, both outwardly and interiorly. The framework, which leads us into deepest mystery and inner reality, consists of a series of symbolic actions, words, songs and gestures, interspersed with moments of reflective silence. All these have evolved over the centuries from the central event of the Last Supper, followed by crucifixion and resurrection, and from the primacy accorded to the Word of God.

Liturgical documents make it clear that the primary symbol at liturgy is the assembled community, gathered to give thanks and praise to our marvelously generous and forgiving God. The assembly's principal "action" is its full, conscious, and active participation in all aspects of the celebration; the actions of standing, kneeling, listening, offering the sign of peace, and processing to the Lord's table are essential components of this participation. Among the actions of the presider are breaking open the scriptures in the homily, leading the community in prayer, and praying for the coming of the Holy Spirit upon the gifts so that they may become Eucharist for us all. Liturgical ministers proclaim the Scriptures, offer bread and cup at the sacred banquet, assist in the sanctuary, and lead the singing. The actions of the assembly, the presider, and the ministers are all symbolic, expressing at each activity a particular aspect of God's creative and redemptive love.

Bread, Wine, and Water

Let us now consider for a moment the symbols of bread and wine, which were used by Jesus himself at the Last Supper, and the wealth of meaning they convey in the preparation of the gifts.

"Blessed are you, Lord, God of all creation," the presider begins, using the form of an ancient Jewish table blessing, the *berakah*. "Through your goodness we have this bread to offer, *which earth has given and human hands have made*. It will become for us the bread of life.... Through your goodness we have this wine to offer, *fruit of the vine and work of human hands.*" Created things, used and formed by humans, will be transformed into the divine. The work of our hands, the thoughts of our hearts, the ministries we do, the words we utter—all will be taken up and offered as the paschal mystery is made present to the assembly. But there is more.

"By the mystery of this water and wine may we come to share in the divinity of Christ, who humbled himself to share in our humanity." We know that this sharing in the divine life is initially brought about by baptism, and deepened through participation in the eucharistic liturgy. But what a stupendous statement this is! We read in the Gospel of John that blood and water flowed from the side of Christ when he was pierced by the lance. This signifies both the divine and human aspects of the church—the one perfect, the other constantly in need of reform. It also symbolizes the incorporation of humanity into Christ in baptism, through the paschal mystery. It is not just the elements of bread and wine and the gifts we offer that are changed during the eucharistic prayer. It is we ourselves—to the extent that we participate in the "sacred mysteries." Thus, at every eucharistic liturgy, we are gradually being transformed into Christ's Body, and we are sent forth to continue his redemptive work in today's world.

The Liturgical Year

An important element of liturgical reform was the mandate to revise the liturgical year so that "the traditional customs and usages of the sacred seasons are preserved or restored to suit the conditions of modern times" (*Constitution on the Sacred Liturgy* 107). Each year, as we journey with Jesus through the events of his life, death and resurrection, these events are made present to us so that we may enter into them and experience the transformation they bring about. As we discussed in Chapter 1, the paschal mystery is an event that impacts us outside of chronological time; it is part of the eternal "now" of God and is therefore present to us today.

Effective Symbols

In order for rituals to really "come alive" for the assembly, the symbols need to make a strong impact on the senses. This is especially true of major celebrations like the Easter Vigil. The new fire should have real flames, and the paschal candle needs to be large and held high for all to see. The whole assembly must process into the church building carrying lighted candles. The Gospel procession should be solemn and ceremonial, with a deacon (or priest if there is no deacon) carrying the Book of the Gospels, accompanied by acolytes carrying lighted candles. There should be a plentiful pouring of water if this is the method of baptism used. Much preferred, however, is immersion in a baptismal bath as advocated by the *Rite of Christian Initiation of Adults* (General Introduction 22), which will emphasize understanding of baptism as a cleansing, a dying and rising. The generous use of oil at confirmation; eucharistic bread that has "the appearance of food" as the 2000 revision of the *General Instruction of the Roman Missal* notes (321); and a beautiful carafe to display the wine—all these help to enliven the liturgical rites. There should be music that everyone can sing and a tastefully decorated worship space (without a super-abundance of flowers more appropriate in a florist shop).

Personal Symbols

Because symbols are so basically woven into human life, many of us have discovered personal symbols that have a special significance for us. Often this significance is related to our experience of God. An example may illustrate: On a wall in our house hangs a framed photograph that my husband, Edward, took in the Pacific Northwest. It shows a small tree that appears at first sight to be growing on a solid rock cliff face. Its bark has been stripped away and its misshapen, gnarled roots are exposed. It has an air of vulnerability, as if its very soul were being unwillingly revealed. Yet the tree clings to life. Closer examination reveals that the root tips have worked their way into fissures and crevices in the rock. The scrawny network of branches bravely flaunt vibrant green leaves. Against all odds, the tree survives.

For Edward, the little tree speaks of the wonder of life—its resilience, its beauty and strength, its sacredness, the work of the Creator's hands. And yet the mystery of life itself cannot be plumbed.

Understanding Symbols

It is sometimes said that a good symbol should be able to stand by itself, without words or explanation. The little tree is a case in point. Certainly, the power of a given symbol depends on its experiential impact at a deeper level than words. Sometimes, however, for this impact to be possible, a simple explanation will be helpful. The significance of the symbolism of water and wine at the presentation of the gifts is a case in point. Such an explanation will need to focus on the *meaning* (historical and/or liturgical) of the symbolic elements, rather than trying to make personal connections to their life experiences.

Many of us have been touched by the story of a developmentally challenged little boy who attended catechetical sessions with other children. We will call him Billy. At Easter time, the group was instructed to bring a seasonal symbol with them to their next meeting, for use in a small ritual. Billy arrived with an empty L'eggs hosiery container. When he brought up his symbol to be placed with the others, he was greeted with jeers. "What is it?" "There's nothing in it." "That's not a symbol!" "Is too," responded Billy. "When they went to look for Jesus, the tomb was empty!" Simple but profound. Easily recognizable to many of us. But those particular children's sensitivity to symbol had not been sufficiently developed, so the meaning needed to be pointed out.

Symbolism and Catechesis

Along with the reform of the liturgy, emphasis on symbolism, such as has been described, has been recovered as from earlier centuries. But many adults are still unaware of the essentially symbolic nature of liturgy, regarding symbols and rituals as "mere externals." They do not realize that ritual is speaking to them on a deeper level than the words that they have been taught.

Given the power of liturgical rites to lead into mystery, it is not surprising that the *Rite of Christian Initiation of Adults* stresses the importance of such rites in the overall formation of those preparing for baptism. A parish catechesis modeled on the catechumenate will emulate this aspect of the process. It will be experiential rather than a series of instructions, though at times some explanation, as outlined above, may be necessary.

In catechetical sessions for children and youth, a brief ritual or special prayer might accompany the bringing of the Bible or lectionary to a place of honor in the learning space. The prayer experience included in the session could be made into a short rite. Alternatively, if the participants make banners or posters illustrated with seasonal or personal symbols, these might be included in a prayer service with an appropriate Scripture reading and perhaps spontaneous intercessions. Simple seasonal rites can easily be created with a little imagination. For instance, as the end of Advent approaches, students could be offered much food for thought with a prayer service, using the "O" Antiphons and symbols they have made—accompanied, of course, by singing!

These few suggestions are just a beginning. No doubt more creative ideas will occur to the catechist as the liturgical year unfolds. These will be growth experiences for him or her as well as for the participants. The important thing is not just the fact that many rituals are used, but that those that are used enable people to enter into mystery. If a symbol does not fulfill that function, it ceases to be symbolic.

In today's pragmatic, frenetic world, it is sometimes necessary to awaken people (adults more than children, who are still more in touch with wonder and spiritual reality) to an understanding of the role rituals and symbols play in our spiritual journey. Some of the settings for adult gatherings lend themselves to an encounter with the symbolic. Before beginning a workshop, I sometimes provide basic art supplies and ask participants to design a simple symbol that expresses their own understanding of a particular aspect of faith. It may be the meaning of the nativity, what inspires them about their favorite saint, or their personal concept of God. Some people relate more easily than others to this type of activity, but for all it results in reflection and the subsequent sharing of their efforts leads to further insights. Appropriate symbols can be used to decorate meeting spaces and other areas of parish activity. Small faith community sessions are an ideal setting for encounters with the symbolic.

Additional Rituals
Within Liturgical Celebrations

Many parishes are already incorporating short, meaningful rituals into liturgical celebrations. Based on the RCIA rite of welcoming for those already baptized and the rite of calling the candidates to continuing conversion, supplementary rituals for sacramental preparation have been introduced. Thus, first communion and confirmation groups, with their parents and sponsors, may be invited before the assembly at one of the Sunday Masses so that they may make a commitment to continuing their faith journey and preparing adequately for the sacraments. Shortly before the respective sacraments are celebrated, another rite may focus on the candidates readiness (their experience of conversion) for these sacraments. Finally, at the celebration itself, participants may walk in the entrance procession, each carrying a lighted candle symbolic of his or her baptism. The candles are then placed in a holder beside the baptismal font.

Worship, as the liturgical documents stress, should be a function of the whole person, not just the physical and cognitive elements of humanness. If we ignore the imaginative and creative aspects—windows that reveal the spiritual and open up limitless horizons—we are ignoring a very vital part of God's gift of life. We are not being fully ourselves. Because ultimately, our goal as humans is to be more closely united to the Source of all being, the Holy Mystery that is the all-loving God.

Discussion Question

For Liturgists and Catechists

- How might representatives of both ministries work together to create meaningful rituals for stages of sacramental preparation?
- How could a particular group in the parish be recognized in a creative way at a Sunday liturgy?

7. Prayer

Discussion Questions

For Catechists

- "There are as many paths of prayer as there are persons who pray" (*Catechism* 2672). To what extent are you presently planning varied experiences of prayer for your catechetical sessions? Do you believe that those present are really being led into an experience of God?
- "Whether we realize it or not, prayer is the encounter of God's thirst with ours. God thirsts that we may thirst for him (cf. St. Augustine, *De diversis quaestionibus octoginta tribus* 64, 4:PL 40, 56)" (*Catechism* 2560). Have you ever thought of prayer in this way? What does this sentence tell you about God? Have you ever experienced a "thirst" for God?

For Liturgists

- Read and reflect on paragraph 2643 of the *Catechism*. In what ways can you help your assembly to appreciate this understanding of liturgical prayer?

The Judeo-Christian tradition has always attached great importance to prayer, both personal and liturgical. So when young or unbaptized children first enter the catechetical process, catechists are rightly eager to teach them to pray. For many, "teaching them their prayers" is a first priority. Initially, however, this may not be the best practice. My own childhood experience may illustrate the reason.

Learned Vocal Prayer

When I was a little girl, I was taught, like countless other Catholic children worldwide, to kneel by my bed each evening and say my night prayers. These were quite numerous—the Our Father, Hail Mary and Glory Be; the Acts of Faith, Hope and Charity; a short examination of conscience followed by the Act of Contrition, and the Angel of God.

Every night I dutifully recited all these prayers, and I did a similar list each morning. Failure to "say my prayers" would have to be mentioned in my monthly confession. But although I understood that praying was "the lifting up of my heart and mind to God" so that I should not recite the prayers mechanically, I found my daily rituals rather tedious. It was hard to concentrate day after day on the same words, trying to make a real, meaningful connection with God through them.

However, besides teaching me my prayers, my mother had told me that God was everywhere, with me always, and that I could talk to God as a friend. Whenever I wished, I could discuss with the Lord my thoughts, feelings, problems, and activities. So after I had finished my set prayers at night, I very clearly remember jumping into bed and conversing with God! From an early age, I started to build a relationship with Jesus and with the Trinity.

Others were probably not so fortunate. For many people, even today, praying means reciting a proliferation of set formulas, perhaps believing that the more prayers they say the better chance they have of receiving a favorable answer to their requests. This is sometimes known as "praying hard." But the *Catechism of the Catholic Church* quotes St. John Chrysostom: "Whether or not our prayer is heard depends not on the number of words, but on the fervor of our souls (St. John Chrysostom, *Ecloga de oratione* 2: PG 63, 585)" (2700).

I remember an elderly sister, a catechist with whom I attended a day of reflection. During a small group session, this sister shared a wonderful discovery she had made that day: "I never realized before," she said, her face aglow, "that I could just talk to God, and that would be praying. I always thought I had to say set prayers." Doubtless, in her long religious life of prayer and service, this good lady had progressed far beyond the recitation of formulae as her only way of praying (even though she did not realize it!). Many people, however, may never do so. Yet it would be hard to find people in a close relationship with one another, still less a couple in love, who made a habit of addressing each other by means of standard pre-established phrases. They may develop some significant phrases to be used on particular occasions, but most of their communication comes spontaneously from the heart.

All this is not to discount the importance of learned vocal prayer, which is a part of our ancient heritage, and teaches us *how* to pray. Rather it is to emphasize the need to internalize the recitation of the prayers we learn. "The memorization of basic prayers offers an essential support to the life of prayer, but it is important to help learners savor their meaning" (CCC 2688 Note the use of the word "savor" rather than "understand"; it suggests leisurely enjoyment.). If meanings are not explained, children may get the idea that to pray is simply to recite memorized words they do not understand. Many of us have had the experience of inviting children to write out the Lord's Prayer, only to be presented with such versions as "Our Father who are in heaven, Harold be thy name" or even "Hello be thy name." To really pray we must enter into the presence of God and engage our hearts in an *attitude of prayerfulness*. Prayer is internalized to the extent that we become aware "of him 'to whom we speak' (St. Teresa of Jesus *The Way of Perfection* 26, 9 in *The Collected Works of St. Teresa of Avila*, tr. K. Kavanaugh, OCD, and O. Rodriguez, OCD [Washington D.C.: Institute of Carmelite Studies, 1980], II, 136) (CCC 2704)."

The Liturgy

The liturgy itself consists mainly of vocal prayers which express the most deeply held beliefs of the people of God. It is a participation in the most perfect and sublime of all prayers, the prayer of Christ himself—the summit of adoration, thanksgiving, repentance, and petition. Yet each person who participates brings to it his or her own personal story, the hopes, desires, joys, and also the pain of life. With these experiences, each person also offers the ministry he or she has performed. All are taken up into the eucharistic mystery, and each person is changed through a personal encounter with the Risen Lord. In the course of this public prayer, there are many moments of silence; times when we can pour forth what is in the depths of our hearts. Participation in liturgy is nourished by daily personal prayer and a deepening relationship with God in Christ.

It is noteworthy that the *Catechism of the Catholic Church* does not say that vocal prayers are sufficient. They are a *support* to the life of prayer. Paragraph 2688 states: "The *catechesis* of children, young people, and adults aims at teaching them to meditate on The Word of God in personal prayer, practicing it in liturgical prayer, and internalizing it at all times in order to bear fruit in a new life."

Besides vocal prayer, the *Catechism* identifies two other "expressions" of prayer: meditation and contemplation. Let us take a brief look at each of these, before suggesting some ways to pray in catechetical sessions.

Meditation

"Meditation is above all a quest" (2705). Our minds try to understand the meaning and demands of Christian living. We desire to grasp what God is asking of us, both as a community and as individuals. Since most of us find sustained concentration difficult, we are helped by the Scriptures, liturgical texts, and the writings of others. There is a very wide variety of methods of meditation, but "the important thing is to advance, with the Holy Spirit, along the way of prayer: Christ Jesus" (see CCC 2706–2708).

Obviously the importance of meditation cannot be over-stressed. In fact, the *Catechism* asserts: "Christians owe it to themselves to develop the desire to meditate regularly" (2707), and it is a preparation for the more intense prayer of contemplation. It is thus of great importance that we introduce this method of prayer to those we catechize, even the very young, and allow many opportunities to practice it.

Contemplation

Contemplative prayer used to be considered the domain of those very few people who were known as "mystics," or at least of cloistered women and men. But Trappist Thomas Merton, one of the foremost writers on prayer and spirituality in the twentieth century, did much to advance the view that contemplation is a gift offered to all Christians.

Contemplative prayer, says the *Catechism*, is "the simplest expression of the mystery of prayer ... a grace [that] can be accepted only in humility and poverty" (2713). It is the expression of the love between God and the forgiven sinner in which the pray-er opens him or herself to the will of God and the transforming love of the Holy Trinity. In contemplative prayer, words are almost totally absent. It is a silent, receptive resting in the presence of God, "a *gaze* of faith, fixed on Jesus" which teaches the "'interior knowledge of our Lord,' the more to love him and follow him (cf. St. Ignatius of Loyola, *Spiritual Exercises*, 104)" (2715).

Like faith itself, contemplative prayer is a gift. Those who are disposed to receive this gift are led by obscure paths into a deeper relationship with God, provided they persevere with discipline and devotion. It is well worth reading and pondering the whole section on contemplative prayer (CCC 2709–2719). Indeed, the whole Part Four of the *Catechism* is devoted to prayer. To read it is bound to enrich the prayer life of anyone who takes time to do so.

"There are as many paths of prayer as there are persons who pray," the *Catechism* remarks (2672). Therefore, a wide variety of prayer experiences need to be introduced in catechetical sessions and other situations where the faith community gathers. The primary purpose of teaching people to pray is to help them grow in their own intimate relationship with Christ and build lives rooted in prayer. But it is also to help them enter more fully and deeply into community worship.

Following is a brief listing of some types of prayer which have been found helpful with groups of varying ages.

Suggestions for Group Prayer

- **Liturgy of the Hours:** The Liturgy of the Hours, or Divine Office, is the only public prayer of the church apart from the eucharistic and other sacramental liturgies. It developed in the early Christian centuries among the desert monks of the early church, and during the Middle Ages it expanded into a series of "canonical hours," each consisting of psalms, canticles, prayers, songs and a Scripture reading. The hours were chanted in monastery churches at set intervals, beginning before dawn and continuing until after sundown. Priests were also required to recite the Office each day. Vatican II mandated that the Liturgy of the Hours should be shortened, reducing the total number of hours to seven, so that it might become the prayer of the whole people of God (see *Constitution on the Sacred Liturgy* 83–101).

  One of these hours, or a shortened version, could be used to open or close a catechetical session. The laity are very much encouraged to participate in this universal prayer of the church, and many parishes celebrate Morning, Evening or Night Prayer regularly.

- **Other Liturgical Prayers:** The psalms themselves may certainly be prayed outside a liturgical context. They contain endless food for thought and are expressions of the deepest human emotions. The more they are prayed, the more meaningful they become. Those being catechized should be given frequent opportunities to dip into this spiritual treasury and be nourished by it. The prayers used both in the eucharistic liturgy and in other sacramental rites often very beautifully focus on particular aspects of faith. An example is the opening prayer of the Mass, especially during the liturgical seasons. It often gives important insights—and therefore food for reflection—into the underlying meaning of Advent, Christmas, Lent, Easter, or the theme of the day.

- **Traditional Catholic Prayers:** The Our Father; Hail Mary; Glory Be; Acts of Faith, Hope, Charity and Contrition; Apostles' Creed; Prayer to the Holy Spirit; and Memorare are prayers that all Catholic children were once expected to learn. Although, as already noted, rote memorization of prayers has little value, traditional prayers should be used from time to time, prayed slowly and reflectively, perhaps with a little meditation added.
- **Prayers of the Saints:** The holy women and men who are included in the Roman calendar (as well as those being considered for canonization) have composed many wonderful prayers over the past twenty centuries. The style and content of these prayers greatly broadens the horizons of those who pray them reflectively.
- **Poetry:** Many Christian poets, and sometimes even non-Christians, have produced inspiring works that may spark new insights. These poems can also be used for prayer and reflection.
- **Spontaneous Prayer:** Spontaneous prayer within a group has not been part of Catholic practice, at least in recent centuries, and many of us feel awkward when we first start praying this way. It takes some practice, but it is well worthwhile, because it gives people an opportunity to pray aloud in their own words and express their feelings freely. Once the catechist has learned to pray spontaneously in a relaxed manner, the people in the group will probably have no problem in doing the same.
- **Devotions:** The Rosary, of course, is part of our Catholic tradition. Many people regard it as *the* essentially Catholic form of prayer and feel an obligation to pray the Rosary each day. This devotion should certainly be

introduced to everyone being catechized. It provides an opportunity to meditate on events in the life of Jesus and on the paschal mystery, while at the same time honoring Mary.

That venerable Lenten devotion, the Stations of the Cross, focuses on the events of the passion and death of Jesus. Today, many meditations and prayers are connected with the Stations, a number of which connect the commemorated events with contemporary social justice and daily life issues.

Devotion to particular saints may be encouraged through prayer, especially on the occasion of their feastdays. A brief introduction to the saint should be offered before the prayer.

- **Prayer with Scripture:** The guided imagery method of prayer is extremely popular with people of all ages. I have used it successfully with young children, as well as with teens and adults. Basically, it is a method that engages the imagination of participants as the catechist or leader slowly leads them into a scene from Scripture and ultimately to a meeting with Jesus. It is necessary to use sensual images ("feel the warmth of the sun," "listen to the voices of the crowd") and to speak slowly, with frequent pauses so that all can place themselves in the scene. When the meeting with Jesus takes place, some quiet time is allowed for personal prayer.

This type of prayer activity may encourage people to try a similar approach to prayer on their own, using the Scriptures and assuming the role of a bystander or even a participant in a biblical scene.

Another method of praying with Scripture, which may be used with teens or adults, is to assign a passage or choice of passages to be read slowly and meditatively. Pray-ers should be instructed to first invoke the enlightenment of the Holy Spirit so that they may be open to whatever God wishes to say to them. They should read through the passage once, then again once or twice much more slowly, until a particular word or phrase seems to "leap off the page" or strike a chord within them. When this happens, it is time to stop reading and start listening to what God is communicating to their hearts, responding appropriately. This is a form of *lectio divina* (CCC 2708) and may lead into the wordless awareness of God's loving presence that is necessary for contemplation.

- **Other Types of Meditative Prayer:** People may be given topics for reflection appropriate to their age and spiritual maturity; they may read or listen to the meditations of others, or they may be given questions for reflection and prayer. Sometimes an object, such as a pine cone, some grains of sand, a sheaf of wheat, or almost anything in nature may be given to participants to contemplate. Perhaps with a little guidance, these items may give rise to new insights and prayer.

Spending meditative time with forests, mountains, lakes, rivers, the ocean, a quiet countryside, or even a small flower garden, can put us in touch with the divine. If the opportunity offers, such prayerful activity may be encouraged for older teens and adults.

There is such a wide variety of prayer forms that it should not be difficult for creative and prayerful catechists and group leaders to introduce something different each week. With this kind of planning, the group will really look forward to this part of the catechetical session. Careful preparation, however, under the guidance of the Holy Spirit, is always necessary. It may be worth emphasizing that whatever the prayer chosen, everyone must understand that it is something that is to engage the whole person, really drawing him or her into an encounter with God. It is not a mere exercise or assignment. "It is the *heart* that prays," the *Catechism of the Catholic Church* says, "the dwelling-place where I am, where I live" (2562, 2563.)

Discussion Question

For Liturgists and Catechists

- The cycle of the liturgical year and its great feasts are also the basic rhythms of the Christian's life of prayer. Are there ways in which your community can be made more aware of the significance of the liturgical year in both public and private prayer?

8. The Catechist

Discussion Questions

For Catechists

- Recall a catechist from your youth (or from your catechumenal experience, if you were initiated as an adult) who played a significant part in your faith journey. What was it about this person that made a lasting impression?
- As catechists, we are called to a vital ministry in the church. What do you think is needed to improve your catechetical skills? How can you integrate these skills into a holistic approach to catechesis?

For Liturgists

- How could you structure an exchange of information and insights between liturgists and catechists, so that each group might better understand the other's ministry? How might such sharing impact liturgies and catechetical sessions in your parish community?

When I first started working on the diocesan level, I spent a lot of time visiting pastors to assess the catechetical needs of their parishes and offer the services of my office. I was always graciously received, and I enjoyed chatting with the priests—some who were old friends and others whom I was meeting for the first time. The visits, however, sometimes showed that catechetical programs might be in need of updating.

Seated comfortably in the pastor's study, a cup of coffee at my elbow, I would ask, "Who is your DRE, Father?" Too often the answer would be, "Oh, we have a good lady who's been doing it for years. She recruits the volunteers and organizes everything."

"What about catechist formation?" I would persist.

"Well, the volunteers are all pretty good Catholics, and we use the "XYZ" series, so they just follow the book."

Of course, there are parishes all over the country where trained Directors of Religious Education place catechist formation at the top of their priority list. But conversations with colleagues, who work in various parts of the United States, suggest that scenarios such as I have outlined above are still not uncommon. The pastors characterized are coming out of an older paradigm, when use of a question-and-answer catechism did not require much training. The faith of the catechist and the fact that his or her own Christian formation had been effected by the same method was regarded as sufficient. Perhaps, when they moved on to a religious education series, these priests had not realized that now "just following the book" without any formation and training was not enough.

What I have said above may be interpreted as criticism. It is not intended as such; rather, it is to emphasize the need for the effective formation of catechists that is called for by the *General Directory for Catechesis*. I certainly have no wish to disparage the efforts either of the pastors or of the good people who have been giving generously of their time for years to "teach children their faith." Most of them are dedicated, sometimes heroic, women and men who have a real love for the children they teach and are genuinely concerned for their spiritual welfare.

The Importance of the Formation Of Catechists, Lay and Ordained

It may at first seem surprising that the *General Directory for Catechesis* identifies "the preparation and formation of catechists in the deep riches of the faith" as the first priority of catechesis (33).

In article 234, the document directs that diocesan programs "must give absolute priority to the *formation of lay catechists*." At the same time, "a fundamentally decisive element must be the *catechetical formation of priests* both at the level of seminary formation as well as at the level of continuing formation." Catechesis is essentially a cooperative effort between clergy and laity. Priests, of course, perform their own vital catechetical work in many settings. Their cooperation and support are also needed in the equally vital ministry of lay catechists.

Catechists and Religion Teachers

We used to think the terms "catechist" and "religion teacher" were synonymous. Even when the *Baltimore Catechism* had been superseded by other texts, the teacher taught the lesson from a book to the class. The material was arranged systematically according to a curriculum with the goal of ensuring that children would *know* all the basic doctrines and moral precepts of Catholicism. The teacher assigned written exercises, passages to be studied, and material to be memorized. Of course, the teacher also gave tests to assess how many facts had been assimilated. A "religion teacher" was regarded by the class as an authority and the expert who knew all the answers.

Although in Catholic schools we claimed that religion was different from all other classroom subjects, the methods employed were often very similar. Even in parish programs, which used to be known as "CCD" and are now many times designated as PSR (Parish School of Religion), the schools model was, and often still is, used.

An important difference between this schools model and the catechetical model we are discussing is that catechists *need not be experts*—in fact, even if they have advanced degrees in theology, they know that there are many questions to which there is no cognitive answer. As has been stressed throughout the book, the primary aim of catechesis is not to instruct in facts but to lead into mystery (the mystery of the God who calls us into intimate relationship and into participation in the very life of the Trinity through Jesus Christ). As has also been emphasized, this is not to deny that a knowledge of basic doctrine is an essential element of the catechetical process.

The Lay Catechist

The *General Directory for Catechesis* explains that the bishop, as the chief catechist, has primary responsibility for catechesis in the particular church (diocese) but that he is assisted by priests, deacons, religious, and laity in communion with him. Each has a particular function within the process, but the *Directory* mainly addresses the needs of lay people who are called to the catechetical ministry. Paragraph 231 states: "The vocation of the laity to catechesis springs from the sacrament of Baptism. It is strengthened by the sacrament of Confirmation. Through [these sacraments] they participate in the 'priestly, prophetic and kingly ministry of Christ' (*Apostolate of the Laity* 26)."

"By sharing the same form of life as those whom they catechize, lay catechists have a special sensitivity for incarnating the Gospel in the concrete life of men and women" (230). The choice of words is important here. "Incarnating the Gospel" is obviously different from just "teaching religion." It implies holistic involvement of the catechist—the way she or he models Gospel values in daily living—particularly in relation to those being catechized.

Human experience is the medium through which the word of God becomes active and grows in each individual person. A similar background, at least in regard to state of life, will make it much easier for the catechist to guide people in recognizing where God is active in their lives. The *General Directory for Catechesis* makes clear that the church's concept of catechesis must be made clear to catechists who do not yet have a full understanding of catechesis as "a school of faith, an initiation and apprenticeship into the entire Christian life" (30). Paragraph 143 adds that catechesis "takes the form of a process or a journey of following the Christ of the Gospel in the Spirit towards the Father" (143).

Dimensions of Catechetical Formation

Obviously, since catechesis is to be a process of formation, not just the passing on of information, catechists themselves must be formed in Christian living. They must grow as disciples of Jesus Christ and members of his Body, as well as being trained in doctrine and teaching techniques.

The *General Directory for Catechesis* cites three "dimensions" of the formation of catechists (238). "The deepest dimension refers to the very being of the catechist, [the] human and Christian dimension." Clearly then, ongoing spiritual growth and each catechist's deepening relationship with God are the foundation of all catechetical formation. The other two dimensions, however, are also of vital importance: "knowing" and "*savoir-faire*." The former refers to all that a catechist is required to know; the latter to an understanding of "those to whom he [sic] transmits the message and of the social context in which they live." An understanding of these factors leads to an informed decision as to how the message may best be presented. These three "dimensions" are closely connected, each interacting with the other two, so that none can be discussed in isolation from the others.

Catechists, who walk with those they catechize on a journey toward transformation in Christ, need to have reflected deeply on the mysteries of faith and related these to their personal faith life. It is their task to help those being catechized discover more deeply who they are. At the core of this discovery process is the experience of the totally accepting and merciful love of God. It is here where we enter into relationship with God.

The Gospel

By interweaving the Gospel story with contemporary, real-life experience, catechists demonstrate that the story is not about events of two thousand years ago, but about today. It is a story that is vibrant and real, and it frequently challenges Christians to turn their values and perspectives upside down, as did the parables of Jesus in his own day.

People in our contemporary culture often set their sights on comfort, security, and living "the good life." They are afraid to take risks. But the well-formed catechist will understand that the Gospel is not about living a comfortable life. Rather it calls everyone to discipleship, a response to the call of Jesus to loving service that at times must risk all, even life itself. It is about "doing this in remembrance of [Jesus]," becoming bread broken and wine poured out for the sake of our brothers and sisters, in whom we see Jesus himself. Again, we see the need for the rooting of catechesis in the liturgy.

If, in our catechetical sessions, we do not present the Gospel as the core of Christian living, the ideal to which all are called, we cannot hope to form disciples of Jesus Christ. Of course, not all those who participate in our sessions will respond to the challenge this presents, just as not all responded to the Lord himself. But some will persevere and grow, proving that the seed was cast on good ground; they will bear fruit abundantly.

Immersion in the Process

Since the baptismal catechumenate is to be the paradigm for all catechesis, it is obvious that the formation process must clearly outline the various elements of the catechumenate. The *General Directory for Catechesis* prescribes that the approach used in catechist formation must be similar to that used in the catechetical process. "It would be very difficult for the catechist ... to improvise a style and a sensitivity to which he [sic] had not been introduced during his own formation" (237). In other words, the "style and sensitivity," even in catechist formation, must be that of the baptismal catechumenate!

My own formation as a catechumenal team member was greatly enhanced by attendance at a number of the Institutes presented by the North American Forum on the Catechumenate, which last from one to several days. The methodology of these Institutes mirrors the process of the catechumenate— breaking open the Scriptures, sharing faith and reflecting on personal life experience. Celebration of the rites of the catechumenate is also modeled.

For most people who attend, a Forum Institute is a wonderful experience of learning by immersion in the process. It is an occasion of grace and spiritual growth. Had I listened to a classroom presentation on the catechumenate for three days or even three weeks, I would have learned very little in terms of the actual process. The whole approach of the catechumenate is based on a dialogue between life experience and the liturgy, particularly the lectionary readings.

Doctrinal Preparation

On the other hand, doctrinal preparation is also necessary. The *General Directory for Catechesis* says, "Sacred Scripture should be the very soul" of this preparation. Along with the Scriptures, the *Catechism* "remains the fundamental doctrinal reference point" (240). This "biblico-theological formation should afford the catechist an organic awareness of the Christian message, structured around the central mystery of the faith, Jesus Christ." It needs to be "of a summary nature and correspond to the message to be transmitted ... [and] ... must be a theological formation that is close to human experience" (241). Therefore, a lengthy, academically oriented program is not required (though the *Directory* does advocate higher education for specialists in catechesis and those who are personally interested in more in-depth theological knowledge).

The *General Directory for Catechesis* further notes that presentations of the "synthesis of faith should be such as to help the catechist to mature in his [sic] own faith and enable him to offer an explanation for the present hope in this time of mission," particularly in view of the "grave and complex problems" (*Christifidelis Laici* 60c) of today's world. In fact, the document asserts, there is "an ever-increasing urgency for doctrinal formation" of all the laity because of these contemporary problems. This is another reason why adult catechesis is now of such basic importance in the church.

The Context of Catechesis

The social, cultural and economic context in which people live greatly impacts their perspectives on life. Therefore, since the message must be relevant to all, catechists need to know the background of those they catechize. A multicultural group will present a real challenge in terms of adequately addressing any perceptual differences resulting from variations in lifestyle and culture. To journey with the group in a loving and compassionate way, the catechist must make the effort to get to know each person and find what "makes them tick." The *General Directory for Catechesis* cites some foundation in the human sciences of psychology and sociology as necessary for the well-rounded formation of catechists (242–243).

Communication Skills

If effective catechesis is to take place, certain practical skills also need to be developed. Of these, communication skills must be singled out as particularly important. Catechists need to be able to share stories of how God has been active in their own lives. This is something that may be difficult at first for those who have always kept their "spiritual" lives private! They must learn how to relate the Gospel and their own experience of Jesus to the lives of others. Catechists must also know how to explain the teaching of the church without becoming too didactic—here, too, human experience must be invoked. The *General Directory for Catechesis* describes the catechist as "essentially a mediator" (156) in the dialogue that takes place between people and "the mystery of God." He or she must be able to facilitate group discussion in which new insights may be expressed, enabling all present to contribute.

Other types of communication skills also need to be learned: how to really *listen* to others and reflect back what has been heard; how to counsel without simply giving advice about what "should" be done in a given set of circumstances; how to deal with problems that may arise in the group while maintaining an atmosphere of respect and loving acceptance.

Catechesis As Continuing Formation

I believe every catechist will agree with the *Directory's* emphasis on the work of catechesis itself as a means of continuing formation (239). Experience, especially if it is evaluated and reflected upon, can help us to "grow in a balanced and in a critical outlook, in integrity, in ... ability to relate, to promote dialogue, to have a constructive spirit, and to engage in group work." Practice "on the job" also helps us to grow in love and respect for the people God brings to our catechetical sessions. We gradually develop an ability to discern the working of the Holy Spirit within each person, to understand deeper meanings that are sometimes cloaked in very ordinary words, to read body language, and to understand how personal circumstances may impact the individual's faith journey.

Diocesan and Parish Formation Programs

In most dioceses, formation programs for parish catechists and catechetical leaders are already functioning. Many award certificates of completion for the various courses they offer. However, in order to reflect the "baptismal catechumenate" model called for by the GDC, changes (possibly substantial) may need to be made in both the content and the methodology presented.

In addition to diocesan formation programs, though, "those of their own Christian community are all important" (GDC 246–247). Among parish formative activities the *Directory* lists:
- fostering an awareness of "being sent by the Church"
- participation in "a catechumenal program designed for young people and adults"
- "immediate preparation for catechesis, done with a group of catechists," including an evaluation of the session afterward
- retreats and various types of classes

The Call to Catechize

The work of the catechist is affirmed in GDC 231 as a "divine vocation" that "confers the mission to catechize. The Lord Jesus invites men and women, in a special way, to follow him, teacher and formator of disciples. This personal call of Jesus Christ and its relationship to him are the true moving forces of catechetical activity." Since this is so, it seems clear that catechists should first respond to this call by preparing themselves as well as possible to fulfill their ministry. Although the formation program I have outlined in this book may seem rather daunting, the importance of the catechetical mission is such that it should be followed as closely as possible.

It is not necessary that formation be complete before a catechist becomes involved in ministry, but it is necessary that formation be ongoing. From the very beginning, though, the volunteer can call on personal experience of sharing faith with others and try to model the values of the Gospel—a most important function of a catechist.

John Paul II has pointed out the powerful truth that we catechize only to the extent that we recognize ourselves as spokespersons of Christ, "enabling [him] to teach with [our] lips" (*On Catechesis in Our Time* 6). So, provided we have prepared ourselves to the best of our ability, we can safely trust that Christ will guide us to do the ministry to which we have been called.

We still need those "good ladies" (and good men), "good Catholics," like those who instructed all those generations of children in the past. In fact, we now need a great variety of people who will be able to catechize children, youth *and* adults of many different ages, cultures, social, and economic backgrounds, forming them as disciples of Jesus. It is the responsibility of each diocese and parish community to make sure that adequate resources are available to provide all these generous people with the formation they need.

Discussion Question

For Liturgists and Catechists

- Since both liturgists and catechists must be involved in the ministry of liturgical catechesis, how do you think each might learn from the other? Should liturgy training include training for the work of catechesis and vice versa?

9. Building and Nurturing A Eucharistic Community

Discussion Questions

For Catechists

- How prominently do your weekly catechetical sessions feature social justice awareness and the call to service? Are these themes clearly related to the liturgical celebration?

For Liturgists

- In your liturgy planning, to which do you assign more importance: orchestrating a beautiful worship experience or facilitating an encounter with God in which the assembly is transformed and sent forth "to love and serve the Lord in each other"?
- In your own life, how has your involvement with liturgy planning helped you in your relationship with God? How has it led you to enter more deeply into the eucharistic mystery?

The concept of community as an essential element of God's salvific plan did not originate with Vatican II. It is, in fact, deeply rooted in the Hebrew Scriptures. It is a people—the Israelites—that God delivers from slavery in Egypt, a people with whom God makes the Covenant through the agency of Moses. The *shema,* the verse from Deuteronomy which every good Jew was to recite daily, begins: "Hear, O Israel! The LORD is our God, the LORD alone!" (Dt 6:4). It is interesting to note that it was not until the time of the prophet

Ezekiel that individual responsibility for sin was recognized (see Ez 18:25–28). Before this, it had always been the people as a whole who had been chastised by the prophets and seen to be punished by God for infidelity to the Covenant. Indeed, although personal culpability was now admitted, the understanding of the whole community as being faithful or unfaithful to the Law continued to prevail until the time of Jesus.

It was with a communal understanding that Jesus established the New Covenant in his blood with the new people of God. This concept has its ultimate origin in the community of the divine persons of the Trinity, the community into which we are all invited by baptism through our incorporation into Christ.

For many years, especially in the United States with its philosophy of "rugged individualism," religion has been regarded as a private matter. Before the Second Vatican Council, we Catholics often saw ourselves as a group of separate entities gathered to fulfill our obligation at Sunday Mass. We may have been friendly to one another, but our prayer was personal rather than shared. Vatican II, however, reaffirmed an ancient vision of inclusivity with its identification of the church as "the new People of God" (*Dogmatic Constitution on the Church* 9). As we have seen, the *Constitution on the Sacred Liturgy* envisaged the liturgy as a celebration by the whole community rather than by a group of individuals. As a sign of this orientation, "We believe" replaced the old "*Credo* (I believe)" of the Tridentine Mass. The eucharistic prayer, although it is spoken by the presider, is an expression of the faith of the assembly ("We offer you, Almighty Father … we ask you … we thank you.") It is as a community that we participate in the paschal mystery, filled with the life of Christ and sent forth to build God's reign.

It is not just as individuals, then, but as a community of faith that we are constantly called to deepen our commitment and grow by using our gifts in the service of others. As we reflect the love of the Father, becoming self-emptying sacraments to one another, Christ comes to presence in the faith community and in the outside world.

Role of the Pastor

The days are long past when it was understood that the pastor would perform all parish ministry (sometimes assisted by dedicated parishioners because "Father needs help"). The Vatican Council's strong emphasis, especially in the *Dogmatic Constitution on the Church* and the *Pastoral Constitution on the Church in the Modern World*, on the role of the laity in the church's mission, has led to redefined roles for both the ordained and the non-ordained. The parish community as a whole, clergy *and* laity, is now perceived as the embodiment of the church in a particular locality, called to continue the ministry of Christ to one another and the surrounding neighborhood.

The pastor has gone from the sole minister in the parish to the leader, initiator, adviser, spiritual guide, and enabler of the community in mission. His ministry is "a service which forms the Christian community ... and strengthens other charisms and services," calling them forth and coordinating them. Priests recognize and promote the dignity of the laity, who share in the common priesthood of the baptized (*General Directory for Catechesis* 224).

As presider and homilist at parish liturgies, the priest plays a key role in the formation and continued growth of the eucharistic community. It is in centering our lives on the eucharistic mystery and extending the liturgical celebration into daily life that we grow, minister, and experience ongoing conversion. Therefore, vibrant liturgies in which the assembly encounters the risen Lord must be the first priority for the parish.

Liturgy Planning

In a parish that is centered on the Eucharist, the liturgy team—priest(s), musicians, ministry coordinator and others—will meet frequently, preferably each week, to plan details of the Sunday celebration in relation to the readings for the week. The priest may outline the content of his proposed homily and invite feedback. Music will be carefully chosen according to the scriptural context, paying attention to the pastoral needs of the assembly and making appropriate musical and liturgical judgments. Suitable banners and symbols, as well as floral or other decoration, will be discussed. Any special ritual that will be included in the celebration that weekend will be carefully planned.

Children's Liturgy of the Word will be a year-long part of parish life. At the end of the introductory rites in the assembly, the younger children are called forward and process out of the church with their catechist. They will hear the proclamation of the readings (usually from a children's lectionary) and an explanation, geared to the age group, by the catechist. There will also be prayer and some kind of activity to reinforce the children's understanding of the day's scriptures. Children return to the larger assembly when the preparation of the gifts begins. It must be emphasized that this weekly experience is not a catechetical but a liturgical one. It enables the small members of the community to participate in the Liturgy of the Word on their own level.

Catechesis

Throughout this book, we have emphasized the inseparable connection between liturgy and catechesis. Catechesis, in all its forms and as the primary expression of the community's mission of evangelization, will always be at the heart of ministry in a liturgically oriented parish. Lectionary-based catechesis of baptized children and teens will continue on a year-long basis (it is not geared to the school year). The parish community will carefully nurture and support all the stages of the initiation process, from initial evangelization through the post-baptismal period of mystagogia, constantly renewing itself in the process. And the Easter Mass that has standing room only will not be one of the later celebrations on Sunday morning. It will be the Vigil.

The pastor, says the *General Directory for Catechesis*, is "the catechist of catechists" (225). It is he who "fosters" the link between catechesis and liturgy and who fosters a sense of community responsibility for the catechetical ministry. He cares for "the basic orientation of catechesis" and integrates it into the wider community mission of evangelization. It is he who discerns "vocations to the service of catechesis" among parishioners and gives "the greatest attention" to the formation of catechetical ministers. His support and enthusiasm are essential to building and maintaining the kind of catechetical ministry that will support and renew the community.

In order to sustain the community's faith journey, it will be necessary to provide a variety of catechetical opportunities for adult members on a continuous basis. These might include scripture study, liturgical formation, spiritual and personal growth activities, doctrinal study, ministry formation presentations, study of social justice issues, and so on. The resources of the wider community, the diocese, local institutions of higher learning, and experts who reside in the locality may be fruitfully tapped for this purpose.

Sacraments

In a community such as we are describing, baptisms (during Sunday liturgies) will be occasions for rejoicing as new members are welcomed into the Body of Christ. As their children grow, parents will be invited to participate as much as possible in catechesis. At the very least, they will discuss with their children the weekly catechetical sessions and share their own adult insights gleaned from the readings. When it comes time for first communion and perhaps confirmation also, parents may be trained to undertake the task of preparation at home, supervised if necessary by catechists. To involve the whole parish, pictures of the children might be posted in the church, and members of the assembly may be invited to become "prayer partners."

In a number of communities, parents are invited to discern, with the pastor or catechist, when their son or daughter is ready for a particular sacrament and when to celebrate with him or her at a Sunday liturgy. This procedure, of course, eliminates the traditional "first communion Mass" and may mean that some teenagers are not confirmed with their peers. But it does allow more flexibility, both for the faith development of the child and for the action of the Holy Spirit.

Marriage preparation is another area in which the parish community can participate, as selected couples are recruited and trained to share with the engaged the wisdom they have acquired over the years.

The Community Supports Its Members

The parish community is a source of nurturing and strength for its members. I remember being scheduled one day to proclaim the Word at a particularly difficult and painful time in my life. As I stood at the ambo, looking out over the assembly, I experienced a sudden sense of warmth and support—even though most of the people there were unaware of my problems. Realization of the bond between us brought me peace and encouragement.

This bonding is characteristic of membership in most faith communities. As an expression of concern for each other's welfare, ministries are set up to meet various needs. The sick and shut-ins are visited, newcomers are welcomed, the elderly are helped with house maintenance chores and offered rides to the church, the doctor's office or the grocery store.

Young couples are supported and encouraged as they become parents for the first time. They are shown how to talk to their children about God and help them form a relationship with Jesus from their earliest days. Couples learn how to develop simple prayer rituals, so that each may make of their home a "domestic church." Here the foundations of faith and practice will be assimilated from the lived example of the parents. In turn, the parents can learn from the simplicity and spiritual openness of their children.

The Parish School

A parochial school is a wonderful part of a parish community and can enrich it in many ways. However, there is sometimes a tendency for teachers, parents, and students to be so involved with school activities that they are perceived to be a separate group, less concerned than others with the wider community. Or, they may be the people who work the hardest in the parish, but their priorities are directed mainly toward the welfare of the school.

If, like catechesis itself, the Catholic education of its children is seen to be the responsibility of the whole parish, such isolation of the school as a separate community will be less likely to happen. Principal, teachers, and parents need to be involved in regular parish activities that are not school-oriented, and families whose children do not attend the school should be involved in school improvement projects or fund-raisers. It is very important, too, that activities in which public and parochial school children participate together are a regular part of parish life.

Inclusivity

It goes without saying that a eucharistic community is inclusive. People of different racial, economic or social backgrounds, different age groups, and sexual orientation are all treated with the dignity due to persons made in the image and likeness of God. All are invited to join the ministry to which they feel called. Provision is made for the optimum functioning of all those with disabilities, and any extra help that may be needed is offered when appropriate.

Small Faith Communities

Perhaps the most fruitful development of all, in terms of sustaining the eucharistic parish, is the formation of small faith communities, also known as basic ecclesial communities. In an atmosphere of prayer and openness, groups of eight to ten people meet regularly to reflect on and discuss the lectionary readings or other appropriate material. They share their faith journeys with one another. They also "assume responsibility for transforming society" (GDC 263–264). Each person brings his or her own unique experience and perspective with which to enrich the gathering. These groups, firmly anchored in the liturgy and drawing strength from it, can form a very strong focus for the whole community. They will be a great unifying element in times of difficulty. Many parishes invite those who have recently entered the church to join such a small community as a means of continuing catechesis.

Outreach

However much we take care of the members of our own parish, this is not enough. As a family is concerned for the welfare of its neighbors, so the parish must reach out to the wider community. If we are to incarnate Christ in our locality as we are called to do, we need to be a visible and active presence. The area in which the parish is situated will suggest the most needed outreach ministries. Is there a prison or juvenile detention center (county, state, or federal) in the vicinity? Are there a number of nursing homes? Is there a poor neighborhood nearby, migrant workers, or refugees, who may be helped in a variety of ways? Perhaps there is need for a literacy program, a soup kitchen, or a health clinic? What about mentally ill people, people with AIDS, or a hospice program that needs volunteers to work with the dying? There may be an interfaith group working in the area to alleviate suffering or fight injustice; joining with them in their efforts would be a great ecumenical gesture that could benefit all concerned.

Ministry, of course, is not only for adults. Even small children may be involved in some way; older children and teens need to minister actively in some capacity. Peer ministry among youth is greatly encouraged and very valuable, but it should not be the only opportunity offered to teenagers. When young people of all ages are involved in the overall mission of the parish, they will come to regard service as an integral part of Christian living, and will become an important element in parish ministries.

Whatever ministries are undertaken, within or outside the parish, there must be a sense of being sent forth as a community. Separate groups "doing their own thing" without reference to the mission of the parish as a whole will not contribute to overall growth of the eucharistic community. There need to be unifying factors: a person who coordinates the efforts of all the ministry groups, and frequent meetings between group leaders. There should also be periodic gatherings of the whole parish community—perhaps for a meal, a picnic, or some other social event—where people can share informally what is going on in their families as well as what they are doing in ministry. Ministries, as a matter of course, will be closely integrated with parish liturgies.

Developing a Eucharistic Community

In many parishes, a eucharistic community such as we are envisaging is already a reality, or is at least taking shape. In numbers of others, there is still a long way to go. A major development of this kind does not come about overnight. It takes much prayer, hard work, and cooperation between all members of the parish. There needs to be time for eucharistic catechesis, for fostering new attitudes, and for planning.

There are many ways to go about developing a community in which the liturgy is understood as being, in concrete terms, the source and summit of the Christian life. One way is to attempt a complete renewal and restructuring of a somewhat lackluster parish within a pre-determined time frame.

The first step will usually need to be a period of intensive catechesis, to ensure that everyone understands not only the liturgy, but how it leads naturally to the formation of a eucharistic community. Enthusiasm will need to be built and the new vision explained to the whole parish. A parish day of reflection or a presentation by a dynamic speaker may be the first step— reinforced by ongoing support from the pulpit each week. Probably a number of community meetings will need to be held, at which a mission statement is developed, relating to the circumstances and location of the parish. Key parish leaders will be identified and trained. A parish survey may be taken to identify the new ministries that need to be added to those already in place.

When the time arrives to implement the overall plan, a ministry fair serves as an effective "sign-up day" for the various ministry groups, representatives of which are on hand to explain needs, goals, and objectives. Leaders will then be selected for each group, formation and training sessions set up, and plans developed for beginning the work itself.

I have known of parishes that have successfully "jump-started" a whole new outlook and a new system of ministries in this way. They have been larger parishes, with a good proportion of younger families. They have had a strong leadership team, headed by the pastor, deacon, DRE, parish council president, and others. All team members have had a good understanding of the underlying concepts of a eucharistic community and its practical application, backed by careful research.

In many cases, however, a more gradual approach will be seen as the most beneficial, taking small steps at a time. For example, after the basic catechesis and preliminary preparation of the community, a process of lectionary-based catechesis might be introduced, formation of catechists undertaken, and small faith communities formed. Ministries already existing in the parish would continue and be encouraged to grow. Increased awareness of the catechumenate process in the parish would be constantly encouraged, and the concept of the eucharistic community would regularly be incorporated into parish liturgies.

A simple way of centering activities on the liturgy is to begin all parish meetings with prayer based on the lectionary readings. Care needs to be taken here, though. I remember attending six meetings in one week where the same scripture passages were read (and even briefly discussed on one occasion.) Together with personal reflection on the Scriptures, small group sharing, leading a catechumenal session, and hearing the word proclaimed on Sunday, this meant that I was exposed to the same passages a total of ten times! Some people might consider this overkill. However, small, creative prayer services that incorporate the themes of the readings could easily eliminate this problem.

The steps outlined in this book are fundamental to the kind of growth we have been discussing. When these innovations seem to be functioning well, new developments might involve parents in sacramental preparation, praying the Liturgy of the Hours (Morning, Evening, or Night Prayer) in the parish, and initiating one outreach ministry to the wider community of the neighborhood. When these practices are established, more ministries within and outside the parish can be introduced.

Throughout the process, parish leadership will need to call forth the gifts of community members and help the people to understand that these are to be used to build the reign of God in their locality. All parish ministries will need to be centrally coordinated to ensure that small, exclusive groups do not develop. The whole enterprise must be undergirded by ongoing prayer.

However a parish chooses to implement the vision, it must always be borne in mind by every member that the objective is not merely to establish a multiplicity of ministries but to build a eucharistic community of faith in which ministries are an essential, practical expression. The liturgy must continue to be at the heart of the community's life—inspiring, empowering, and transforming the effort of each community member for the life of the world.

"While the liturgy daily builds up those who are within into a holy temple of the Lord, a dwelling place for God in the Spirit, to the mature measure of the fullness of Christ, at the same time it marvelously strengthens their power to preach Christ and thus shows forth the Church ... as a sign lifted up among the nations" (*Constitution on the Sacred Liturgy* 2). A truly eucharistic community will always be such a sign.

Discussion Question

For Liturgists and Catechists

- Since liturgical catechesis requires collaborative ministry, discuss how parish liturgy committee members and catechists could together form a small faith community for sharing faith. How do you think this might contribute both to community liturgies and to the catechetical process?

Bibliography

Official Documents

Congregation for the Clergy. *General Directory for Catechesis*. Washington, D.C.: United States Catholic Conference, 1997.

Connell, Martin, ed. *The Catechumenal Documents: A Parish Resource*. Chicago: Liturgy Training Publications, 1996.

Flannery, Austin. *Vatican Council II: The Conciliar and Post Conciliar Documents*. Northport, N.Y.: Costello Publishing Co., 1981.

Hoffman, Elizabeth, ed. *The Liturgy Documents: A Parish Resource*. Chicago: Liturgy Training Publications, 1992.

International Commission on English in the Liturgy. *Rite of Christian Initiation of Adults*. Chicago: Liturgy Training Publications, 1988.

John Paul II. *On the Coming of the Third Millennium*. Washington, D.C.: United States Catholic Conference, Inc., 2000.

Lysik, David A., ed. *The Liturgy Documents: A Parish Resource*. Vol. 2. Chicago: Liturgy Training Publications, 1999.

National Conference of Catholic Bishops. *Our Hearts Were Burning Within Us: A Pastoral Plan for Adult Faith Formation in the United States*. Washington, D.C.: United States Catholic Conference, 2000.

United States Catholic Conference, Inc. *The Catechism of the Catholic Church*. Washington, D.C.: United States Catholic Conference, 2000.

Recommended Reading

Baronowski, Arthur R. *Creating Small Faith Communities: A Plan for Restructuring Parish Life*. Cincinnati: St. Anthony Messenger Press and Franciscan Communications, 1995.

Barry, William. *Prayer As Personal Relationship*. Mahwah, N.J.: Paulist Press, 1994.

Bernstein, Eleanor, ed. *Children in the Assembly of the Church*. Chicago: Liturgy Training Publications, 1993.

Birmingham, Mary. *Word and Worship Workbook, Year A*. Mahwah, N.J.: Paulist Press, 1998.

———. *Word and Worship Workbook, Year B*. Mahwah, N.J.: Paulist Press, 2000.

———. *Word and Worship Workbook, Year C*. Mahwah, N.J.: Paulist Press, 1997.

Cooke, Bernard. *The Future of the Eucharist*. Mahwah, N.J.: Paulist Press, 1997.

Dorr, Donal. *Integral Spirituality: Resources for Community, Peace, Justice and the Earth*. Maryknoll, N.Y.: Orbis Books, 1990.

Duffy, Regis. *Real Presence: Worship, Sacraments and Commitment*. San Francisco: Harper & Row, 1982.

Duggan, Robert D., and Maureen A. Kelly. *The Christian Education of Children*. Mahwah, N.J.: Paulist Press, 1991.

Edwards, Pamela J. *Catechizing with Liturgical Symbols*. San Jose: Resource Publications, Inc., 1997.

Feider, Paul A. *The Sacraments: Encountering the Risen Lord*. Notre Dame, Ind.: Ave Maria Press, 1986.

Fleischer, Barbara J. *Facilitation for Growth: A Guide for Scripture Study Groups and Small Christian Communities*. Collegeville, Minn.: Liturgical Press, 1993.

Heney, David. *Motivating Your Parish to Change: Concrete Leadership Strategies for Pastors, Administrators, and Lay Leaders*. San Jose: Resource Publications, Inc., 1997.

Horan, Michael P., and Jane E. Regan. *Good News in New Forms: A Companion to* The General Directory for Catechesis. Washington, D.C.: National Conference of Catechetical Leadership, 1998.

Jorgensen, Susan S. *Rekindling the Passion: Liturgical Renewal in Your Community*. San Jose: Resource Publications, Inc., 1993.

Mahony, Roger. *Gather Faithfully Together: Guide for Sunday Mass*. Archdiocese of Chicago: Liturgy Training Publications, 1997.

McBrien, Philip J. *Lectionary Index for the* Catechism of the Catholic Church. San Jose: Resource Publications, Inc., 1995.

Mongoven, Anne Marie. *The Prophetic Spirit of Catechesis*. Mahwah, N.J.: Paulist Press, 2000.

Morris, Thomas H. *The RCIA: Transforming the Church*. Mahwah, N.J.: Paulist Press, 1989.

Nichols, Vincent. *The Gift of the Mass*. Mystic, Conn.: Twenty-Third Publications, 1997.

Richter, Klemens. *The Meaning of Sacramental Symbols*. Collegeville, Minn.: The Liturgical Press, 1990.

Shannon, William H. *Exploring the* Catechism of the Catholic Church. Cincinnati: St. Anthony Messenger Press and Franciscan Publications, 1995.

Turner, Paul. *The Catechumenate Answer Book*. ML Answers the 101 Most-Asked Questions. San Jose: Resource Publications, Inc., 2000.